FOUR-DIMENSIONAL JESUS

*Seeing Jesus Through the Eyes of
Matthew, Mark, Luke, and John*

FOUR-DIMENSIONAL JESUS

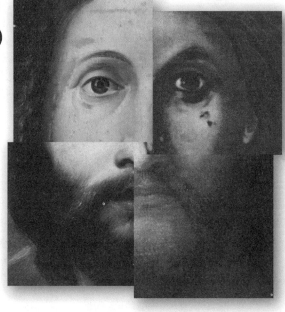

*Seeing Jesus
Through the Eyes of
Matthew, Mark,
Luke, and John*

JOHN TIMMER

CRC Publications
Grand Rapids, Michigan

Library of Congress Cataloging-in-Publication Data
Timmer, John, 1927-
    Four-dimensional Jesus: seeing Jesus through the eyes of Matthew, Mark, Luke, and John / John Timmer.
      p. cm.
    Includes bibliographical references.
    ISBN 1-56212-532-X
    1. Jesus Christ—Biography.   2. Bible. N.T. Gospels—Criticism, interpretation, etc. I. Title.
    BT301.2.T55 2001
    232.9'01—dc21

                                     00-054878

10 9 8 7 6 5 4 3 2 1

CONTENTS

FOREWORD

Matthew, Mark, Luke, and John—each of these four gospels was written in a different part of the world. Each addresses a different Christian community. Each presents a different portrait of Jesus. Together they offer a rich plurality of portraits.

But almost from the beginning, having four separate portraits was perceived as a problem. Soon the church felt a need to "harmonize" the four portraits in order to present Jesus from a single perspective. Thus around the year A.D. 175 a Syrian Christian by the name of Tatian set out to merge the four gospels into one and produce a harmonized gospel, free from all differences and discrepancies. What the church needed, Tatian believed, was a single story of Jesus rather than four different ones. Using a cut-and-paste method, he wove the four New Testament gospels into a seamless narrative. The end project—the *Diatessaron*—was enormously popular and was used in the Syrian area for a couple of centuries. Fortunately, better judgment eventually prevailed, and the church rejected the *Diatessaron* in favor of the four gospels that this harmony had tried to replace.

The *Diatessaron* may have disappeared, but the spirit that produced it lives on. Even today, efforts to fashion one gospel out of four continue. Having four gospels, after all, presents serious problems. What are we to make of their differences? One harmonized narrative conveniently erases such differences—and problems. And who among us is innocent of harmonizing the narratives? For example, at our Christmas services we place the shepherds and the wise men in the same stable. But the shepherds and the wise men belong to different gospels. Luke's shepherds visit the stable; Matthew's wise men go to the house where Joseph and Mary live. Or consider a typical Good Friday service. The so-called "seven words" from the cross are presented as though Jesus uttered them one after the other. If things were only that simple. Mark's gospel has only one last word: "My God, my God, why have you forsaken me?" In Mark, Jesus utters a single cry and dies feeling forsaken by God. Not so in John's gospel, in which Jesus dies with a shout of triumph: "It is finished." Now, if Jesus' words in Mark and John are presented as sequential, in a harmonized reading, we are left wondering, How did Jesus die? In agony or in triumph? Besides, we will have difficulty feeling the horror of Jesus' death that Mark portrays and feeling the power of Jesus' triumphant cry that John shows.

The church has always come out in favor of multiple portraits of Jesus over a single harmonized portrait. It has done so in spite of considerable divergence among the gospels. Confessing with Paul that "we have this treasure [called Jesus] in jars of clay" (2 Cor. 4:7), the church has embraced the plurality of gospels.

In the chapters that follow we will explore the differences of the four gospels. We will see how an understanding of these differences leads to a four-dimensional portrait of Jesus, a portrait richer, though more complex, than the single, harmonized portrait that Christians sometimes produce.

ONE JESUS, FOUR PORTRAITS

Gospels. What are they? Biographies of Jesus? If so, why do they pay so little attention to things that are dear to a biographer's pen? Why do they display minimal interest in the biographical data of Jesus' life? Strikingly, the gospels offer no description of Jesus' personal appearance. They contain virtually nothing about his family background. They are silent about his education. They make little attempt to date his actions. The gospel of Mark, for one, tells us nothing about these things. It also does what no biographer would do: skip over the first thirty years of Jesus' life. So, by and large, do the other three gospels.

If the gospels are not biographies, what are they? They are writings reporting the good news that Jesus is the Messiah. The gospels were written "that you may believe that Jesus is the Christ [that is, the Messiah], the Son of God, and that by believing you may have life in his name" (John 20:31). Yet each of the four gospel writers presents this good news in a unique way. The Jesus who appears in their gospels is an *interpreted* Jesus. Guided by the Holy Spirit, each writer paints a distinctive portrait, arranging the stories and sayings of Jesus to focus on the spiritual needs of a particular community.

Mark's Portrait of Jesus

Until the late nineteenth century most scholars believed that the gospel of Mark was simply a pale imitation of the gospel of Matthew. Mark, after all, contains very little that is not found in Matthew as well. And Matthew is almost twice the length of Mark. Saint Augustine (354-430) called Mark the abbreviator and follower of Matthew, and Augustine's description stuck. Through the centuries Matthew tended to be the most read and Mark the least read of the gospels. This situation began to change in the second half of the nineteenth century. Careful study of the gospel texts revealed that things were just the other way round: Mark had not used Matthew; rather, Matthew had used Mark. This discovery triggered a fresh reading of Mark. Mark was no longer seen as an imitator of Matthew. Mark, in fact, was the first to paint a written portrait of Jesus.

Mark's Opening Line

"If there had never been a Christian religion, if Jesus had disappeared from memory, if there was no Matthew, Mark, Luke or John, and, one day, we discovered a little book which opened with the line *The beginning of the gospel of Jesus Christ, the Son of God*—what would we think? Our brains are dulled with familiarity. Even if, from an early age, you have rebelled against the whole idea of God and religion, you will have heard the name of Jesus Christ. You will have heard the description 'the son of God.' You will know the word *gospel*. . . . And so it is very hard to imagine hearing or reading for the first time 'The beginning of the gospel of Jesus Christ, the Son of God. . . .' But it is probably the most stunning opening line ever written. It is the start of St. Mark's Gospel."

—Alec McCowen, *Personal Mark,* New York: Crossroad, 1984, p. 9.

Who Is Jesus?

Of the four gospels, Mark alone centers from beginning to end on the problem of Jesus' identity. At the outset Jesus is an unidentified stranger and an unfathomable mystery. As the story progresses, the question on everybody's lips is, "Who is this?" The crowds, the scribes, the high priest, Jesus' relatives and disciples—they all ask it.

Who is Jesus? Mark tips his readers off in the opening sentence of his gospel: "The beginning of the gospel about Jesus Christ, the Son of God." So Jesus is the Christ. He is the anointed one, for that is what the name Christ means. In the Old Testament the one who is anointed is above all the king, which prompts the question, If Jesus is the anointed King, when will he be acclaimed as King? When will he be crowned? When will he ascend his throne and rule? This question draws readers into Mark's story and keeps them in suspense.

Who is Jesus? For the benefit of his readers Mark briefly answers this question in the opening sentence of his gospel: Jesus is the Messiah, the anointed King. But none of the people within his gospel knows this. All they know is that Jesus is different from anyone else. No one knows what accounts for the difference.

Jesus' Secret

In Mark, Jesus refuses to declare openly who he is. Only in one place (8:27-33) does he come near to admitting that he is the Messiah, the anointed King. Everywhere else he seeks to hide his identity as the Messiah, wishing to conceal a secret about it. The secret is this: the Messiah must suffer. The Messiah is not a triumphant but a humiliated figure.

When Jesus asks the disciples, "Who do you say I am?" and Peter answers, "You are the Messiah," Jesus warns them not to tell anyone. Then he quickly shifts from the title Messiah to the title Son of Man, teaching the disciples that the Son of Man must suffer many things and be rejected and killed (8:31). Although he does not explicitly reject the title Messiah, Jesus prefers the title Son of Man. For Mark, Jesus is the Messiah who hides himself and chooses to express his identity as the Son of Man.

Of course, to openly claim the title Messiah would have been to court wholesale misunderstanding, because the title Messiah referred to the highest political office in Judaism. The Messiah, a descendant of David, was to rule Israel in the same way as King David. He would defeat the Romans, liquidate Gentile opposition, and lead Israel to a position of world leadership. Understandably, Jesus hurries to distance himself from this political role by calling himself the Son of Man. By claiming this title, Jesus indicates that he knows that he must suffer, yet one day God will bring him out of defeat to triumph.

Jesus' announcement that the Messiah must suffer and die shocks Peter. To him and the other disciples, a suffering Messiah is a contradiction in terms. Yet this contradiction, Mark shows, is at the heart of Jesus' mission.

Following Jesus

For Mark, the focus of Jesus' life is the cross. Mark makes the shadow of the cross fall over nearly one-half of his gospel. The Jesus he portrays is above all the suffering Jesus. Mark emphasizes this aspect of Jesus' ministry more than any of the other gospels. And why? Because suffering is so much part of the life of the Christians in Rome to whom he most probably writes. In A.D. 64, Emperor Nero accused these Christians of setting fire to the city of Rome. As a result, many Roman Christians were killed. Mark is writing a pastoral response to this crisis, and in his gospel these Christians discover that nothing they are suffering is alien to Jesus. The Jesus they meet in Mark stands before them "in the glare of the fires lit by Nero" (W. D. Davies) and calls them to take up their cross and follow him.

Matthew's Portrait of Jesus

Who Is Jesus?

Like Mark, Matthew portrays Jesus as the Messiah, though he emphasizes the secrecy of Jesus' messianic identity less than Mark does. Almost as soon as he appears, Matthew's Jesus is welcomed as the promised one of Israel's history. As the heir of David and of Abraham (1:1-17), his mission is first to Israel: "He will save his people from their sins" (1:21). Yet Jesus' mission field is much wider than Israel. In fact, it embraces all nations. This is why Matthew tells the story of the Magi from the east. Their visit foreshadows the day when east and west will bow before the "king of the Jews" (2:2).

Matthew's Church

The church for which Matthew writes his gospel is apparently a church in transition. Its life is painfully marked by change and confusion. For although the church's original members had been mostly Jewish, its current members are mostly Gentile. And this major shift from a Jewish Christian to a Gentile Christian membership called for rethinking the meaning of the Jesus stories as told, for example, in the earliest gospel, the gospel of Mark. "A remodeled church needs a remodeled gospel," says John P. Meier in *The Vision of Matthew.* "Matthew, the faithful servant of the tradition, wishes to affirm, not reject, his Christian past. But he knows that *his* situation is different and that consequently the tradition must be understood in a new light" (p. 28).

To resolve the tension between past Jewish and current Gentile membership, Matthew presents Jesus from a different perspective than that to which the original Jewish membership had been exposed. With a written form of Mark's gospel in front of him, Matthew sets out to rework and remodel it. He incorporates about 80 percent of Mark's gospel into his own and generally follows Mark's story outline. Still, his overall portrait of Jesus is quite different from Mark's. Though Matthew is a faithful guardian of the Jesus tradition, he is not a mechanical copier. By adding from sources other than Mark and using a process of reordering and rewriting, Matthew makes old traditions speak with a fresh voice to changing conditions.

> **Matthew, the Most Used**
>
> "It is the only gospel that uses the word 'church.' Of all the gospels it was best suited to the manifold needs of the later church, the most cited by the church fathers, the most used in liturgy, and the most serviceable for catechetical purposes. . . . The evangelist we call Matthew had a genius for collection and organization that made his gospel the best guide to practical Christian life."
>
> —Raymond E. Brown, *The Churches the Apostles Left Behind*, New York: Paulist Press, 1984, p. 124ff.

Jesus the Teacher

Mark presents Jesus primarily as the incognito Messiah destined to suffer and die, but Matthew presents Jesus first and foremost as the teacher of the church. He does this by structuring his gospel around five large discourses of Jesus' teachings and by inserting these discourses into the story outline borrowed from Mark. The five discourses are these:

1. *The Sermon on the Mount* (*chapters 5-7*). In this sermon Jesus is the teacher of Christian morality. The clue to understanding this morality is grasping that the one who teaches it also embodies it. Jesus is what he teaches. Jesus lives what he teaches. To do what Jesus teaches in the Sermon on the Mount, we must possess the Christ-like qualities mentioned in the opening beatitudes (5:3-11). We must be poor in spirit, meek, merciful, pure in heart, and makers of peace.

2. *The Mission Discourse* (*10:5-42*). Here Jesus commissions the twelve apostles to proclaim by word and action the approach of the kingdom of God. His words apply not just to the twelve disciples; they are equally valid for all who will be enlisted in the service of the kingdom in years to come.

3. *The Parable Discourse* (*13:1-52*). In the seven parables of this discourse, Jesus teaches that the kingdom progresses in secret. In the first and most important of these parables—that of the sower—he teaches that the

kingdom is coming like vulnerable seed that birds can devour, thorns can choke, and the sun can scorch. And Jesus is the sower of that seed. In him the kingdom of God enters our world. To those who know this, these parables are revelations about Jesus. To those who don't, these same parables are puzzles or mystifying conundrums.

4. *The Discourse on Church Order* (18:1-35). The question "Who is the greatest in the kingdom of heaven?" triggers this discourse. The answer: those who are meek and humble of heart, for they imitate the essential attitude of Jesus. Thus the church is well-ordered when leaders and members humble themselves.

5. *The Eschatological Discourse* (24:1-25:46). In this final discourse Jesus teaches about the end of the world and his return in glory. The question he keeps asking is, When I come, will I find you watching and ready?

At the end of Matthew the risen Jesus refers to all five discourses when he commissions his disciples to "go and make disciples of all nations . . . teaching them to obey everything I have commanded you. And surely I will be with you always, to the very end of the age" (28:19-20). These words provide the key to understanding Matthew's whole gospel. They tell us that, in contrast with Jesus' ascending from his church in Luke 24:51, the risen Jesus comes to his church as its teacher and will abide with it until the end of the age.

Luke's Portrait of Jesus

Who Is Jesus?

It is widely believed today, writes Joseph A. Fitzmyer, that Luke wrote his gospel for a Gentile Christian audience. His readers "were not Gentile Christians in a predominantly Jewish setting; they were rather Gentile Christians in a predominantly Gentile setting" (*The Gospel According to Luke I-IX*, p. 59). To address this audience, Luke portrays Jesus as bringing salvation to the whole world and creating a worldwide community in which the distinction between Jew and Gentile is irrelevant.

Luke starts off by setting his story in the context of world history. Jesus is born in Bethlehem because Caesar Augustus has decreed "that a census should be taken of the entire Roman world" (2:1). Jesus' genealogy is traced back to Adam (3:38), the forefather of all humankind, and not simply to his Jewish ancestors, David and Abraham (as in Matthew). Luke never raises the question of whether Jesus is sent only to the Jews, as Mark and Matthew do in the story of the Syro-Phoenician woman. And when Jesus is brought to trial, Luke's interest focuses on the proceedings in the Roman court, not, as in Mark and Matthew, on the proceedings in the Jewish court. Luke shows that Jesus' innocence was established before a Roman court—a world court. Luke's worldwide perspective flows from his belief that Jesus' mission is worldwide. He begins his gospel with Simeon's announcement that the infant Jesus is "a light for revelation to the Gentiles" (2:32) and ends it with the risen Jesus reminding his disciples "that repentance and forgiveness of sins will be preached in his name to all nations" (24:47). There can be no question, writes W. D. Davies, "that for Luke the greatest fact of the first century was the church in which the division between Jew and Gentile had been annulled" (Invitation to the New Testament, p. 224).

First Sermon

In Luke, Jesus reveals his identity in his inaugural sermon in the synagogue of Nazareth, his hometown. The story of this event, in a way, contains the whole of Luke's gospel. It gathers into itself all the events that follow. In the Nazareth synagogue Jesus proclaims his mission: to bring in God's year of Jubilee—the year that is to see the end of poverty, bondage, and oppression. Jesus begins his sermon with a quotation from Isaiah 61:1-2: "The Spirit of the Lord is on me, because he has anointed me to preach good news to the poor. He has sent me to proclaim freedom for the prisoners and recovery of sight to the blind, to release the oppressed, to proclaim the year of the Lord's favor."

At first Jesus' listeners respond with enthusiasm. They marvel at his gracious words and speak well of him. But when he applies the passage to himself, they start having doubts. "Isn't this Joseph's son?" In the end, after Jesus hints at the inclusion of Gentiles within God's purpose of salvation from oppression, the people of Nazareth run him out of town. That is because, in his sermon, Jesus refers to two Old Testament events to show that already, centuries ago, God had been gracious to the Gentiles. When there was a great famine, the prophet Elijah was not sent to any of the widows in Israel, but only to a Phoenician widow. And the prophet Elisha healed none of the lepers in Israel, but only Naaman the Syrian. What Jesus is saying is this: Because the people of Nazareth reject him as the fulfiller of Isaiah 61:1-2, he is now forced to offer salvation to the Gentiles, just as Elijah and Elisha did in their day. In other words, at the very beginning of his ministry, Jesus already sees himself as the bringer of salvation to the whole world.

Breaking Down Barriers

Luke, A Piece Torn from Wildness

"Luke is the most reasoned, calm, plausible, and orderly Gospel. . . . But Luke's Gospel is calm and plausible only compared to the swirling bewilderments of Mark and the intergalactic leapings of John. All of the Gospels are unprecedented, unequaled, singular texts. Coming at Luke from our world, we stagger and balk. Luke is a piece torn from wildness. It is a blur of power, violent in its theological and narrative heat, abrupt and inexplicable. It shatters and jolts. Its grand-scale, vivid, and shifting tableaux call all in doubt."

—Annie Dillard, "The Gospel According to Saint Luke," in *Incarnation*, New York: Viking, 1990, p. 29.

Luke focuses his portrait of Jesus more sharply by telling numerous stories of Jesus accepting people whom the Jews held in contempt. For example, the Jews loathed tax collectors who willingly had contact with Gentiles and who had a well-deserved reputation for dishonesty and extortion. They equally loathed the Samaritans, whom they considered racial and religious half-breeds. So it comes as no surprise that Luke, rather than the other gospels, tells the parables of the Good Samaritan (10:25-37) and of the tax collector (18:9-14). Nor is it surprising that only Luke records the story of Jesus' stay at the house of Zacchaeus the tax collector (19:1-10). With these stories Luke shows that Jesus' all-embracing love breaks down barriers to prepare for the worldwide church.

John's Portrait of Jesus

Jesus, says Mark, is Messiah Incognito, the great unknown. Jesus, says Matthew, is the teacher of the church. Jesus, says Luke, is the inaugurator of a worldwide community in which the distinction of Jew and Gentile has become irrelevant. Who does John say that Jesus is?

The One Who Is Sent

The gospel of John offers many answers to the question of Jesus' identity. No other gospel presents such a wide array. In the first chapter alone, Jesus is named the Word, the Lamb of God, the Messiah, the Son of God, the King of Israel, and the Son of Man. And in John, Jesus makes no effort to deny or qualify any of these identities.

Among the many designations in John, however, the one that stands out is Jesus' self-designation as the one sent from the Father. It is Jesus' fundamental understanding of himself. Coming from the Father and being sent by the Father distinguishes Jesus from everyone else. Jesus represents the Father, speaks for the Father, acts on the Father's behalf. Jesus is no mere prophet, the way John the Baptist was. He carries the Father's authority. Writes Jose Comblin, "The Father did not send Jesus to bring a gift to humanity; he sent Jesus to humanity. . . . Jesus, in the Fourth Gospel, is solely and entirely he who was sent. His whole being is a communication between God and the world" (*Sent from the Father,* New York: Orbis Books, 1979, p. 2ff.) Jesus does not bring a message from the Father; he is the message. Jesus does not reveal truths; he is the truth. Jesus does not offer bread from heaven; he is that bread. Jesus does not impart life from above; he is the life. Jesus is not the bearer of divine light; he is the light. "I am the light of the world," Jesus tells the Pharisees—who immediately challenge him to prove it. Jesus answers them: "I am one who testifies for myself; my other witness is the one who sent me—the Father" (8:18). John's entire gospel is based on the understanding that Jesus comes from the Father and that everything he says and does flows from his oneness with the Father. Jesus descended from the Father and testifies to what he has seen and heard with the Father.

John's Sole Concern

"John is concerned with one theme only, which he continually varies: to know him is life. That, then, is the one question that he asks his readers: Do we know Jesus? Everything else fades into twilight and darkness; it loses its importance and is pushed aside."

—Ernst Kaesemann, *Jesus Means Freedom,* Philadelphia: Fortress Press, 1969, p. 146.

The Four Gospels Compared

"Mark sees Jesus from beneath, historically, in all his rich humanity, transparent to the mystery of deity. Matthew sees Jesus in profile, doctrinally, highlighting Jesus' head (as Rembrandt does with Paul) so that we especially see Jesus' powerful thinking and teaching. Luke is a study of Jesus' hands and, behind the hands, a study of the heart that moved the hands into a ministry to all kinds of people but especially to outsiders, the marginal, and the disdained. . . . John is a portrait of Jesus from above, from the eagle's eye, revealing Jesus to us in all his majestic preexistent deity, visible now palpably in human flesh. . . . Still another way to see the Gospels comparatively is to say that in theological form Mark is Luther, Matthew is Calvin or Thomas [Aquinas], Luke is Wesley or Xavier or Chrysostom, and John is Augustine or Barth."

—Frederick Dale Brunner, *The Christbook,* Waco, Tex.: Word Books, 1987, p. xvii.

SESSION 2

BORN OF MARY

The stories of Jesus' birth are among the best-known stories in the Bible. They appear, however, in just two of the gospels, Matthew and Luke. Mark, the earliest of the four gospels, has no birth story of Jesus. Mark begins with the man Jesus going to the River Jordan to be baptized. John, the latest of the four gospels, also has no birth story. John traces Jesus' origin to "in the beginning," before creation. If you've read the story of Jesus' birth in Luke, you may think you also know the story recorded in Matthew. But you'd be wrong. For although the stories of Matthew and Luke do include much of the same material, there are significant differences. The lists below provide a summary of similarities and differences of the two gospels.

Similarities

1. The virgin Mary conceives Jesus through the power of the Holy Spirit (Matt. 1:18, 20; Luke 1:35).
2. Mary does not conceive Jesus through intercourse with Joseph (Matt. 1:20, 23, 25; Luke 1:34).

3. Mary and Joseph are engaged to be married, but are not yet living together (Matt. 1:18, 25; Luke 1:27, 34).
4. Joseph descends from David (Matt. 1:16, 20; Luke 1:27; 2:4).
5. An angel announces the conception and forthcoming birth of Jesus (Matt. 1:20-23; Luke 1:30-35).
6. An angel instructs that the child must be named Jesus (Matt. 1:21; Luke 1:31).
7. An angel announces that Jesus will be the savior (Matt. 1:21; Luke 2:11).
8. Jesus is born after Joseph and Mary have begun living together (Matt. 1:24-25; Luke 2:5-6).
9. Jesus is born in Bethlehem (Matt. 2:1; Luke 2:4-6).
10. Jesus is born during the reign of King Herod the Great (Matt. 2:1; Luke 1:5).
11. Jesus grows up in Nazareth (Matt. 2:23; Luke 2:39).

Differences

1. Matthew's genealogy (1:1-16) opens his gospel and introduces the story of Jesus' birth. Luke's genealogy (3:23-38) is part of the story of Jesus' baptism. Matthew begins the genealogy with Abraham and traces the line forward to Jesus. Luke reverses the order. He begins with Jesus and traces back to Adam.
2. None of the events reported in Matthew 2 are in Luke 1-2. The visit of the magi, the massacre in Bethlehem, the flight into Egypt, the return to Judea, and the continued flight to Nazareth are found only in Matthew. And most of Luke 1 and 2 has no parallel in Matthew. The story of Elizabeth and Zechariah, the birth of John the Baptist, the census bringing Joseph to Bethlehem, the adoration of the shepherds, and the presentation of Jesus in the temple are found only in Luke.
3. In Matthew, Joseph is the main focus; the angel's announcement of Jesus' birth comes to him. In Luke, the announcement comes to Mary, the virgin and highly favored one, while Joseph stands on the sideline.

The Emperor Myth

The beginning of wisdom in understanding the infancy stories in both Matthew and Luke lies in being aware of their contemporary context. This context is the "emperor myth." Writes Ethelbert Stauffer, "For millennia there was handed down among the wise men of the east the myth of the divine king who would redeem creation from its primeval curse. For millennia the guardians of the ancient myth searched the stars in order to learn the day of the redemptive epiphany. Generations came and went. Then there arose the age of the great emperors, whose brightness streamed from the Roman west far out into the east" (*Christ and the Caesars*, p. 15). First-century wise men were convinced that a new era had begun with the Roman emperor Augustus. The divine and the human, they believed, had become one in the person of the emperor. The emperor would be the one to lift the curse from the earth and bring worldwide salvation.

Caesar Augustus

"*Caesar* was only one of the titles Augustus bore. Others were *rex, imperator, princeps, pontifex maximus* and so on. He ruled Rome and thus virtually the whole civilized world. He was worshiped as a god. People burned incense to him. Insofar as he is remembered at all, most people remember him mainly because at some point during his reign, in a rundown section of one of the more obscure imperial provinces, out behind a cheesy motel among cowflops and moldy hay, a child was born to a pair of up-country rubes you could have sold the Brooklyn Bridge to without even trying."

—Frederick Buechner, *Peculiar Treasures*, New York: Harper & Row, 1979, p. 18.

But the imperial myth soon proved to be a mixed blessing. Caesar Augustus, founder of the Roman Empire and ruler of the Mediterranean world at the time of Jesus, was indeed able to bring peace for the first time in anyone's memory, and for that he was honored and worshiped as divine. But the peace he brought, the so-called *Pax Augusta*, was a peace imposed by military might and oppression.

And then suddenly a different star appeared. It pointed to Jerusalem. Wise men from the east followed the star and, aided by interpreters of the Jewish scriptures, found the child who had been born "King of the Jews," and worshiped him. Herod quickly responded to this rival power, ordering soldiers "to kill all the boys in Bethlehem and its vicinity who were two years old and under" (Matt. 2:16).

Though Herod claimed to be king of the Jews by the grace of Israel's God, he was actually king by the grace of the Roman Senate. Roman legions had helped him to conquer Palestine. As a lackey of Rome, his job was to maintain law and order, imple-

Herod's Message to Jesus

"You cannot rule men by love. When you find your king, tell him so. Only three things will govern a people—fear and greed and the promise of security. Do I not know it? Have I not loved? I have been a stern ruler—dreaded and hated—yet my country is prosperous and her borders at peace. But wherever I loved, I found treachery—wife, children, brother—all of them. Love is a traitor; it has betrayed me; it betrays all kings; it will betray your Christ. Give him that message from Herod, King of Jewry."

—Dorothy L. Sayers, *The Man Born to Be King*, Grand Rapids, Mich.: Eerdmans, 1943, p. 35ff.

ment imperial policy, and defend Roman interests. To finance his army, his fortresses, multiple palaces, building projects, gifts to imperial figures, and tribute to Rome, Herod bled his people dry by extorting outrageous taxes. To stay in power, he set up a police state, complete with loyalty oaths, secret police, informers, and swift imprisonment, torture, and death for political dissenters.

To understand both Matthew and Luke, we must read them against the backdrop of this imperial myth. The ultimate question both gospels ask is this: Who rules the world? Who is king of all the earth? Caesar Augustus or Jesus? Who is the legitimate king of the Jews? Herod or Jesus? Does this king side with the powerful, the conqueror, and the oppressor? Or with the powerless, the conquered, and the oppressed?

The Genealogies of Jesus

The emperor myth, for example, provides the sinister background music of Matthew's genealogy from start to finish. It is already heard in the opening line, "A record of the genealogy of Jesus Christ the son of David." Matthew's first concern in the opening chapter of his gospel is to demonstrate that Jesus, not Herod, is the true king of Israel—descended from King David through Joseph.

Notice too that Matthew doesn't state that Mary is of the tribe of Judah or of the house of David. The only information we have about Mary's lineage is found in Luke 1, where Elizabeth is said to be a descendant of Aaron and therefore of a priestly line within the tribe of Levi (1:5) and a relative of Mary (1:36). This means that Mary is of levitical, perhaps of Aaronic, descent. Actually, writes John P. Meier, from the New Testament point of view "any consideration of Mary's lineage is beside the point. The Jewish milieu out of which the Infancy Narratives came regularly traced a child's genealogy through his or her father, whether or not the 'father' was actually the biological parent. . . . Hence the lineage of Joseph is what determines the lineage of Jesus" (*A Marginal Jew,* vol. 1, p. 217). And the point of affirming that Jesus is descended from David is that, in Jesus, God fulfills the promise he made to David: "I will raise up your offspring to succeed you, who will come from your own body, and I will establish his kingdom. He is the one who will build a house for my Name, and I will establish the throne of his kingdom forever. I will be his father, and he will be my son" (2 Sam. 7:12-14).

Matthew comments on this divine promise in 1:17: "Thus there were fourteen generations in all from Abraham to David, fourteen from David to the exile to Babylon, and fourteen from the exile to the Christ." Here Matthew divides the history of Israel into three periods: the period before the kingdom of David, the period during the kingdom of David, and the period after the kingdom of David. With Jesus' birth, Matthew is saying, the kingdom of David is here again; the King who will occupy the throne of David forever has arrived.

How does Matthew's genealogy compare to Luke's? The most important thing to keep in mind here, according to Raymond Brown, is that "genealogies serve different purposes and that an individual can be accorded two or more different genealogies according to the purpose for which they were drawn up" (*The Birth of the Messiah*, p. 65). This observation helps us solve at least some of the problems we run into when we place the two lists of names side by side. Since Luke, unlike Matthew, includes the period from Adam to Abraham, his list has seventy-seven names compared to Matthew's forty-one. But even in the period where both genealogies overlap (between Abraham and Jesus), Luke's has fifty-six names compared to Matthew's forty-one. The period between Abraham and David (some 750 years) is the only area where the two genealogies agree extensively. In the following period, that from David to the Babylonian exile (some four hundred years), the two lists differ almost entirely. Here Matthew chooses descendants of David who were reigning kings, and Luke chooses descendants who were not reigning kings. In the period from the Babylonian exile to Jesus (some 575 years) the two lists agree only in the first two (Shealtiel and Zerubbabel) and in the last two names (Joseph and Jesus).

The two genealogies have different functions. The purpose of Matthew's genealogy is establishing that Jesus is the son of David. But Luke has an entirely different purpose. Luke's genealogy is not part of the infancy narrative, but comes after the story of Jesus' baptism when a heavenly voice declares, "You are my Son, whom I love; with you I am well pleased" (3:22). The purpose of Luke's genealogy is to trace Jesus' lineage back to Adam and to God himself, and so reaffirm the words of the heavenly voice in the baptismal story, "You are my

Genealogies: Bore or Boost?

"In the exile Israel told stories of rootage and belonging. It recited genealogies. To outsiders these genealogies seem a tedious bore, but to insiders they are an index for locating rootage. The genealogies are a guarantee that Israel is not adrift in a vacuum of this present generation but has security and credentials. And as long as Israel can name names, utter their precious sounds, it has a belonging place which no hostile empire can deny."

—Walter Brueggemann, *The Land*, Philadelphia: Fortress Press, 1977, p. 145ff.

Son." Despite differences in function, both genealogies must be read against the background of the imperial myth.

Matthew's Story of Jesus' Birth

Matthew's story is like a musical score. It has an upper clef and a lower clef. To tell the full story we must sound both simultaneously. The lower clef tells the earthly part of the story: Jesus has many forebears, including a mother called Mary and a father called Joseph. The upper clef tells the heavenly part of the story: Jesus' mother is "with child through the Holy Spirit" (1:18); Jesus' father is informed about this in a dream (1:20-21). Both clefs combine to produce the story of Jesus' birth.

In the genealogy that precedes the story, Matthew includes the names of four women: Tamar (1:3), Rahab (1:5), Ruth (1:5), and Bathsheba (1:6). These four names are unexpected. Rather than mention the four wives of the patriarchs (Sarah, Rebekkah, Leah, and Rachel), Matthew mentions these four women, each of whom represents some "irregularity" in salvation history. All four are foreigners. Yet God implanted them into David's line and recognized them as legitimate links in the genealogy stretching from Abraham to Jesus. Matthew 1:18-23 (the story of Jesus' birth immediately following the genealogy) is saying that the supreme "irregularity" is Jesus— for he is not of Joseph's seed and therefore is not a descendant of David. To remedy this situation, the angel encourages Joseph, who is a descendant of David, to make the son of Mary a son of David. Despite the fact that Jesus is virginally conceived through the Holy Spirit, Jesus only qualifies as a son of David because Joseph, who is a "son of David" (1:20), accepts him as his son and so engrafts him in David's royal line.

To Matthew, engrafting Jesus into David's line is God's will. Hadn't an angel from God ordered Joseph to take two steps to ensure Joseph's legal paternity? And hadn't Joseph done exactly as the angel of the Lord had commanded him? In taking Mary home as his wife, Joseph had publicly assumed responsibility for the mother and for the child about to be born. And in calling the child Jesus, Joseph had accepted the child as his own. By naming the child, writes Raymond Brown, "Joseph acknowledges him as his own. The Jewish position on this is lucidly clear and is dictated by the fact that sometimes it is difficult to determine who begot the child biologically. Since normally a man will not acknowledge and support a child unless it is his own, the law prefers to base paternity on the man's acknowledgement" (*The Birth of the Messiah,* p. 139). By exercising the father's right to name the child, Joseph had become the legal father of Jesus and Jesus had legally become the son of David. Joseph's action had opened up the way for the fulfillment of God's promise to King David that "your house and your kingdom will endure forever before me; your throne will be established forever" (2 Sam. 7:16). So the unfolding story of Jesus' birth in Matthew also supports his genealogy.

Echoes of Balak

If in Matthew 1 the music of the imperial myth is barely audible, in Matthew 2 it blares out through the voice and actions of King Herod. The basic theme of Matthew 2 is the resolve of Herod to kill the child Jesus, an immediate threat to his royal power. In the report of the magi, Herod correctly senses the longing among eastern people to throw off Roman imperialism and restore native rule. Reading the story of Herod and the magi, we cannot help but hear echoes of the story of Balak and Balaam (Num. 22-24). Here the people of Israel are about to enter the Promised Land. They are camping in the country of Moab whose King Balak fears them and seeks to destroy them. Balak enlists Balaam, a pagan diviner from the east, to help him: Would you please curse my enemies? But Balaam, instead of cursing Israel, three times blesses them and then prophecies the future greatness of Israel and the rise of its royal ruler: "A star will come out of Jacob; a scepter will rise out of Israel. He will crush the foreheads of Moab" (Num. 24:17).

There are striking parallels between the Balak story and the Herod story:

- As Balak seeks to use a diviner from the east to destroy his enemies, so Herod seeks to use magi from the east to destroy his enemy.
- As Balaam foretells that a star symbolizing the Messiah will rise, so the magi see the star symbolizing the Messiah at its rising.
- As Balaam "got up and returned home" (Num. 24:25), so the magi "returned to their country" (Matt. 2:12).
- As God protects Israel against the curse, so God protects the Christ child from being killed by the sword.

All these echoes of the Balak story remind us that God, rather than blocking the path of evil people like Balak and Herod, ordinarily works through their evil deeds, bending their designs to his sovereign purpose.

Luke's Story of Jesus' Birth

When we leave Matthew's birth stories and enter Luke's, it seems as though we are stepping into a different world. And in a sense we are. In Luke's stories we are entering the world of the Old Testament. Poems, hymns, prayers, and stories combine to create an Old Testament atmosphere. The reader is made to feel at home. Here there are no magi, no King Herod, no massacre of the Bethlehem innocents, no flight into Egypt. Here we find stories of the birth of John the Baptist, the songs of Mary and Zechariah, the surprise appearance of angels to shepherds, the circumcision of Jesus, and the presentation in the Temple. But as in Matthew, here too the point of the story is the birth of a king. Luke's story, nevertheless, "is less explicit and graphic about how the birth of Jesus as the new king of Israel stands in direct opposition to the established rule of Herod and Caesar" (Richard A. Horsley, *The Liberation of Christmas,* New York: Crossroad, 1989, p. 23ff.). True, Caesar Augustus is mentioned, but as an agent of God who by imperial decree brings Jesus to Bethlehem to be born. And while an atmosphere of fear pervades Matthew 2, we find celebration and doxology in Luke 2. In Matthew, Jesus is born into a politically hostile world. In Luke, he is born into a worshiping community where Mary sings the *Magnificat,* Zechariah the *Benedictus,* Simeon the *Nunc Dimittis.* But even though political conflict seems far away, even here we find opposition. As in Matthew, the point of Luke's story is the birth of a King who stands in direct opposition to royal and imperial power. In Luke, for example, the angel tells Mary that Jesus is the one to whom the Lord God will give the throne of his father David and who will reign over the house of Jacob forever (Luke 1:32-33). Thus, Luke is saying, God is declaring Jesus the new King and announcing the death of Herod's power and, by implication, of imperial power.

Or listen to Mary in Luke 1:51-52: "He has performed mighty deeds with his arm; he has scattered those who are proud in their inmost thoughts. He has brought down rulers from their thrones but has lifted up the humble."

This is revolution. It's bad news for the world's power brokers. The child to whom I will give birth, Mary sings, will be the agent of radical reform. He will liberate people from political oppression and economic depression. He will change the face of human society. Mary's song undermines the power of the ruling class. It declares the bankruptcy of the imperial myth. And if you have difficulty believing that this is going to happen, Mary sings, then look at me. For I am living proof. In me, God has stooped as low as he can to exalt me as high as he can. And what has happened to me is what will eventually happen to the world at large. When the child in my womb is born, all things will be turned upside down. Those at the top will end up at the bottom; those at the bottom will end up on top. The reversal will be universal.

We miss the point of Mary's song if we read it as applying only to Mary. Mary's words describe social patterns: lowly groups are raised up and groups now on top are cast down. God's agenda is not just about forgiving sins and justifying sinners. It is also about exalting the oppressed and feeding the hungry. And so confident is Mary that God will do these things that she uses the past tense. Mary sings as though what shall be has already happened: God *has* brought down rulers from their thrones; God *has* lifted up the humble; God *has* filled the hungry with good things; God *has* sent away the rich empty. Mary uses the past tense even though many of the meek are still at the bottom and many of the proud at the top. Mary knows that the God of Israel won't allow this to go on forever. He will establish a societal order in which the arm of oppressors will be broken and the meek will rule.

In Luke, the story of Jesus' birth is a reversal story. It announces the bankruptcy of imperial power and the birth of infant power. Power has slipped out of the hands of kings and emperors and moved into the hands of a child. The rod of oppressing rulers has been shattered and a child has been put in charge. To see that this has actually happened, we need the eyes of someone like Simeon. When Mary and Joseph bring Jesus to the temple,

---

Pharaoh, Caesar, Hitler

"The terms 'Pharaoh,' 'Caesar,' and 'Hitler' . . . identify forces to which we must say No, and . . . the reason for this is that Pharaoh and Caesar and Hitler share a common ambition—they all want to be God; that is to say, they all demand the unyielding loyalty that belongs to God alone. 'Give us a blank check,' they insist. 'Don't hold us accountable to anything or anyone beyond ourselves. And if you try to do so, or threaten us in any way, we will dispose of you.'"

—Robert McAfee Brown, *Saying Yes and Saying No,* Philadelphia: Westminster Press, 1986, p. 58.

Simeon tells Mary, "This child is destined to cause the falling and rising of many in Israel, and to be a sign that will be spoken against, so that the thoughts of many hearts will be revealed" (Luke 2:34-35). Simeon is quoting from Isaiah 8. Jesus, he is saying, will present people with an ultimate choice, a choice none of them can escape. Jesus is either a rock of salvation or a rock of stumbling. We are either saved by this child or judged by him. The ultimate authority does not belong to Caesar but to the Jesus child.

HERALDED BY JOHN

I nitial contact with Jesus, all four gospels agree, is indirect. To reach Jesus we must go through John the Baptist. Before we can come to terms with Jesus, we must first come to terms with John the Baptist. But this poses a problem. John is not an appealing character. He reeks of wild zeal. He is a grim prophet of fiery judgment. He's eager to take on the establishment. For starters, his birth contradicts established medical knowledge that barren women "well along in years" cannot have babies. John also upsets the established practice of priestly succession. He turns his back on the obligation to follow in his father's footsteps and continue the family's priestly line. Forsaking tradition and family duty, John disappears into the wilderness of Judea, where he preaches divine judgment and how to escape it. Had there been newspapers in John's days, a headline in the *Jerusalem Post* might well have read "Sole Son of Temple Priest Turns Wilderness Weirdo." Finally, John's baptizing activity gets him into trouble with the temple establishment. By offering a baptism of repentance for the forgiveness of sins, John is in effect saying, I offer in baptism what you have been normally getting through temple sacrifices. With both the temple and John claiming to make people acceptable to the Lord, how can the two not be rivals? There's no question: John is a problem.

Where Shall We Put John?

"There is an old anecdote told about the minister who was preaching on the subject: 'Where shall we put John?' In great detail he discussed first whether to put John in the old covenant and then went on to ask whether he could be put in the new covenant. Finally, an old countryman stood up in the church and said: 'Put him here, for I'm going!'"

—Bo Reicke, *The Gospel of Luke,* Richmond: John Knox Press, 1964, p.51.

So what moves Jesus to identify with John the Baptist? Why does he submit to John's baptism? Why does Jesus join the Baptist in trying to center Jewish life on a new rite that lacks the sanction of temple authorities? Why, like John, does Jesus offer "forgiveness to all and sundry, out there on the street, without requiring that they go through the normal channels"? (N. T. Wright, *The Meaning of Jesus*, p. 39). To answer these questions we must take a closer look at the various portraits the gospels present of John.

Mark's Portrait of John

Mark sees John as fulfilled prophecy. In the opening statement of his gospel he applies to John a quotation from Isaiah 40 that speaks of the new exodus, which was foreshadowed by the exodus from Egypt. This new exodus also calls for a way through the wilderness, but this time the wilderness is located in the human heart. The way is repentance—repentance needing outward confirmation through baptism in the river Jordan. As in Egypt many centuries ago, so now all Israel—"The whole Judean countryside and all the people of Jerusalem" (1:5)—leave their homes and travel to the place where Israel of old crossed over into the promised land. Again they must "cross" the Jordan, although now symbolically and inwardly, to enter upon a new land of promise where the glory of the Lord is about to be revealed in Jesus of Nazareth.

Strikingly, Mark's portrait of John says less of John's baptizing and preaching than it does of John's garb and diet: "John wore clothing made of camel's hair, with a leather belt around his waist, and he ate locusts and wild honey" (1:6). Why such detailed attention to John's clothes and diet? To have us identify John as the prophet Elijah. John's clothing is like Elijah's (2 Kings 1:8); his diet is like a wilderness nomad's. Though Mark does not say so explicitly, his point is clear: John is the end-time messenger described in Malachi 4:5-6. Before that great and dreadful day of the Lord comes, Malachi writes, Elijah will come and "turn the hearts of the fathers to their children." And Jesus confirms that role, referring to John as the one who comes first and restores all things (9:11).

In Mark's portrait, then, what John says and does seems to matter less than who he is. The simple fact that John is on the scene can only mean one thing: the end is near. John's brief two-sentence message supports this. Each of the two brief sentences anticipates the end: "After me will come one more powerful than I" and "I baptize you with water, but he will baptize you with the Holy Spirit" (1:7-8).

John the Watchdog

"John the Baptist has always seemed to me like the Doberman pinscher of the gospel. In the lectionary, he always appears right before Christmas, when no one's defenses are up. Here we are trying to get to the stable in Bethlehem. We are not hurrying. We have set a respectable pace, and with just weeks to go it really is in sight—that starlit barn where everything is about to happen. It is right up ahead there, with people gathering around it, and for those of us who love it, it is all we can see. We aren't thinking about the few dark blocks that still separate us from it when all of a sudden—GRRROW-ROW-ROW!!!—this big old dog with a spiky collar has got us by the ankle. 'Repent, for the kingdom of heaven has come near.' Before he is through, our heads are pounding with vipers, wrath, axes, and unquenchable fire, when all we really wanted was a chance to sing "O Holy Night." . . . John is the watchdog who makes sure no one wanders into holy precincts unaware."

—Barbara Brown Taylor, *God in Pain*, Nashville: Abingdon Press, 1998, p. 22.

Matthew's Portrait of John

If Mark's identification of John as the Elijah to come is implicit, Matthew's is explicit.

Matthew identifies the two most clearly in the story of Jesus' transfiguration. The disciples ask Jesus, Is it true, as the teachers of the law say, that Elijah must come first? Jesus answers, It is true; in fact, he has already come—he is John (17:10-13).

On another occasion Jesus tells the crowd, "If you are willing to accept it," John the Baptist "is the Elijah who was to come" (11:14). But why "if you are willing to accept it"? Why is this so hard to accept? Why this "if you are willing to accept it"? Because John the Elijah and Jesus the Messiah stand or fall together. Identifying John as the Elijah to come presupposes the identification of Jesus as the Messiah to come. John is not Elijah as such; he is the Elijah of the Messiah.

Matthew also clearly relates John, the end-time Elijah, to the kingdom of God. In Matthew, John belongs to the period of the *new* kingdom. John preaches the same message as Jesus: "Repent, for the kingdom of heaven is near" (3:2; 4:17). The period of Old Testament promise continues up to John, and his ministry begins the period of fulfillment. Hence, Jesus says, John is more than an Old Testament prophet (11:9). He inaugurates the kingdom, he lives in kingdom time: "From the days of John the Baptist until now, the kingdom of heaven has been forcefully advancing" (11:12). Like Jesus, John preaches the kingdom.

Gorbachev Is Coming

"If you want an idea of John the Baptist, there were thousands of them when Gorbachev came to New York. They were playing John the Baptist roles—straightening out the streets, keeping the traffic away, causing the 'Gorby Gridlock'—that sort of thing. But that's exactly what they were doing. A potentate was coming—a leader of state—and they prepared the way for that."

—William J. Bausch, *Timely Homilies*, Mystic, Conn.: Twenty-Third Publications, 1990, p. 74.

Luke's Portrait of John

A Spirit-filled Prophet

In Luke, Elijah is not so much the new Elijah of Malachi 4:4-5 (the prophet sent from God before the great and dreadful day of the Lord to turn the hearts of the fathers to their children) as the epitome of the Spirit-filled prophet. Luke portrays John as the one against whom all other prophets are to be measured. Thus, the angel appearing to John's father says that John "will go on before the Lord, in the spirit and power of Elijah, to turn the hearts of the fathers to their children" (Luke 1:17). The angel unmistakably refers to Malachi 4:4-5, yet does not identify John as the Elijah who will restore all things. John, he says, will be *like* Elijah—a mighty prophet of repentance. In Luke, the restoration of all things takes place with the coming of Christ at the end of history and not with John's coming. Jesus, says Luke, "must remain in heaven until the time comes for God to restore everything, as he promised long ago through his holy prophets" (Acts 3:21). In contrast to Mark and Matthew, Luke's John is simply and solely the forerunner of the Messiah and the inaugurator of the messianic age (16:16). He is the first preacher of the gospel (3:18) and is the prototype of the Christian evangelist.

John Ranks Below Jesus

Most of Luke's material on John the Baptist appears in the birth stories. Actually, Luke describes John's birth in surprising detail. The background for understanding Luke's account lies in Acts 19:1-7. In this story Paul is in the city of Ephesus in Asia Minor. Here he meets a group of about twelve men who claim to have received the baptism of John the Baptist. After Paul explains the difference between John's baptism and Christian baptism, he rebaptizes them, laying on hands so that they receive the Holy Spirit. This story provides evidence that one of the rivals the early church faced was the community that sprang from the ministry of John the Baptist, a community whose followers had spread beyond the boundaries of Palestine. Disciples of John who became Christians confessed that Jesus was the Messiah and that John was his forerunner. Those who did not become Christians, however, resented John's being reduced to a secondary role. Their resentment led the early church to rigorously subordinate John to Jesus.

The church's stance is reflected in Luke's account of John the Baptist, particularly in the birth stories of chapters 1 and 2. These two chapters compare throughout the conception and birth of John and Jesus. As the following columns show, the comparison is surprisingly detailed:

John the Baptist (Luke 1)	Jesus (Luke 1-2)
1. The parents are introduced	1. The parents are introduced
2. They expect no child because mother is barren	2. They expect no child because unmarried
3. The angel Gabriel appears	3. The angel Gabriel appears
4. Zechariah is troubled	4. Mary is troubled
5. "Do not be afraid"	5. "Do not be afraid"
6. Your wife shall bear a son	6. You will give birth to a son
7. You shall call him John	7. You shall call him Jesus
8. He will be great before the Lord	8. He will be great
9. Question: How can I be sure?	9. Question: How will this be?

10. Answer: reprimand by angel
11. Sign: You will be silent
12. Response: Zechariah is speech-less because of unbelief
13. Departure of Zechariah
14. Birth, rejoicing, circumcision and naming of John, with accompanying wonders
15. Greeting of child John by inspired Zechariah; growth of child

10. Answer: revelation by angel
11. Sign: Elizabeth is pregnant
12. Response: Mary yields to word of God
13. Departure of the angel
14. Birth, rejoicing, circumcision, and naming of Jesus, with accompanying wonders
15. Greeting of child Jesus by in-spired Simeon and Anna; growth of child

Why does Luke devote so much space to John the Baptist in what, after all, is Jesus' nativity story? The answer is that the comparison is deliberately composed to demonstrate Jesus' superiority over John. For example, John's parents may be upright in the sight of God, but Jesus' mother Mary is the highly favored one. John's mother, though old and barren, may conceive her son naturally, but Mary conceives her son virginally. John's birth may be published among neighbors and relatives, but Jesus' birth is published by a host of angels. John is circumcised at home, but Jesus is circumcised in the temple. John is described as becoming strong in spirit, but Jesus is said to grow in wisdom and stature and in favor with God and people. In these comparisons Luke's purpose is to show that Jesus ranks far higher than John.

John on the World Stage

Of the four gospels, Luke places John on the widest stage. John the Baptist, says Luke, initiates a new movement, not just in the history of Israel but also in the history of the world: "In the fifteenth year of the reign of Tiberias Caesar—when Pontius Pilate was governor of Judea, Herod tetrarch of Galilee, his brother Philip tetrarch of Iturea and Traconitis, and Lysanias tetrarch of Abilene—during the high priesthood of Annas and Caiaphas, the word of God came to John, son of Zechariah, in the desert. He went into all the country around the Jordan, preaching a baptism of repentance for the forgiveness of sins" (3:1-3).

John appears on the world stage, along with one emperor, three tetrarchs, and two high priests. And the movement John is initiating is diametrically opposed to the reality symbolized by Tiberias Caesar. This movement introduces norms and values that are clearly on a collision course with those of the Roman empire. The word of God introducing this new movement does not come to any of the world's power elite. It does not come to those who have the power to decide who will live and who will die, who will be at the top and who at the bottom. It does not come to those who define reality as a closed world where everything is settled. The word of God breaks into the human scene, not in Rome or Jerusalem, not in a palace or the temple, but in the Judean desert.

In this way Luke sets the stage for the coming worldwide conflict between the political and religious power brokers and the word of God. The reality championed by Tiberias and his political allies is closed and fixed. It forbids revolutionary words. It locks John the Baptist up in prison (3:20).

Opposing this reality is John, preaching "a baptism of repentance for the forgiveness of sins" (3:3). John's baptism initiates the dismantling of the world of Tiberias and his underlings, a world essentially organized against grace and therefore an unforgiven and unforgiving world. Forgiveness inevitably leads to another way of organizing human society. Forgiveness rehabilitates the marginalized and the outcasts. It creates new beginnings. In short, forgiveness redefines reality. So the baptism of John "is a radical word which shakes heaven and earth. . . . The world is an exiled, unforgiven world. Tiberias and his counterparts have made it so and keep it so. [John's] strange wilderness word is that forgiveness might reconstitute the world" (Walter Brueggemann, "Luke 3:1-4," in *Interpretation,* October 1976, p. 409).

John Baptizes Jesus
(Mark 1:9-11; Matt. 3:13-17; Luke 3:21-22)

The Baptism Downplayed

Each of the first three gospels begins its account of Jesus' ministry with his baptism by John the Baptist. Mark simply reports the baptism without any explanation for why the sinless Jesus submits to a baptism meant for sinners. Matthew and Luke, however, make efforts to downplay the significance of the event by putting it in soft focus. In Matthew, John the Baptist demurs when Jesus presents himself to be baptized. Jesus has to convince John. John says, "I need to be baptized by you and do you come to me?" Jesus replies, "Let it be so now; it is proper for us to do this to fulfill all righteousness." Luke's approach is more radical than Matthew's. After telling of John's imprisonment for preaching judgment to Herod, Luke briefly, almost in passing, mentions that Jesus was baptized. Luke doesn't say who baptized Jesus. We assume it is John the Baptist, but then can't help wondering how this can be, seeing that John is already in prison. The fourth gospel takes the most radical approach of all. It never mentions Jesus' baptism. Nor does it ever call John "the Baptist" or connect John's baptism with repentance and sin. In the fourth gospel John's main function is not to baptize Jesus but to witness to Jesus.

As we read the story of Jesus and John the Baptist in the four gospels, starting with Mark (the earliest gospel) and ending with John (the latest), we clearly sense that first-century Christians felt a growing measure of discomfort about the baptism of Jesus. Why, so they wondered, did the sinless Jesus need a baptism for the forgiveness of sins? Didn't Jesus himself take away the sins of the world? Then, didn't Jesus' baptism place John in a position superior to Jesus? It's likely, therefore, that to keep John from overshadowing Jesus, the early Christians placed Jesus' baptism in increasingly softer focus.

The Spirit Descends on Jesus

The climax of Jesus' baptism occurs when Jesus comes up out of the water, sees heaven being torn open and the Spirit descending on him like a dove, and hears a voice from heaven declare, "You are my Son, whom I love; with you I am well pleased." This theophany, or manifestation of God, takes up most of the baptismal story in each of the first three gospels. For it's not the baptism itself but the theophany that follows that identifies Jesus. It anoints Jesus with the Holy Spirit to the office and work of the Servant of the Lord. As the kings of Israel were anointed and so became the Lord's Anointed (1 Sam. 16:13); as also the priests were anointed for their office (Ex. 29:7); and, above all, as the Old Testament figure of the Servant of the Lord was anointed with the Spirit of the Lord (Isa. 11:2; 42:1; 44:3; 61:1), so also Jesus, the end-time King, Priest, and Prophet, is anointed with the Spirit of the Lord. And this scene of Jesus' anointing is charged with the fulfillment of Old Testament prophecies. The words "You are my Son" echo Psalm 2:7-8: "You are my Son; today I have become your Father. Ask of me, and I will make the nations your inheritance, and the ends of the earth your possession." The words "with whom I am well pleased" echo Isaiah 42:1: "Here is my servant, whom I uphold, my chosen one in whom I delight; I will put my Spirit on him." From the moment the Spirit descends on him, Jesus knows that he is enlisted into God's service and that God has designated him to inaugurate the time of salvation. As a result, Jesus attaches supreme importance to his baptism. Once, when asked by religious authorities, "By what authority are you doing these things?" Jesus replies, "John's baptism—was it from heaven, or from men? Tell me!" (Mark 11:28-30). Jesus is saying that his authority rests on the theophany at the time of his baptism.

Baptized to Die

The story of Jesus' baptism gives an initial answer to the question, Who is Jesus? Jesus' baptism in the Jordan prepares for Jesus' death. In his baptism, Jesus is acting out his impending death, for to Jesus, baptism means death. In Mark 10:38, for example, Jesus speaks of his death as a baptism: "Can you drink the cup or be baptized with the baptism I am baptized with?" he asks James and John. Then as he moves steadily toward the cross, he says, "I have a baptism to undergo and how distressed I am until it is completed" (Luke 12:50). Jesus' death on the cross is his baptism. His baptism by John is the first public announcement of his death. By submitting to John's baptism, Jesus announces that he has come to die. Jesus goes down under the water of the Jordan to act out his coming death. We should also remember that Jesus comes up out of the water to act out his coming resurrection.

The Fourth Gospel's Portrait of John

As the portrait of Jesus in the fourth gospel is quite different from those in the first three gospels, so is the portrait of John the Baptist. This is immediately apparent. In the opening chapter John is starkly contrasted to the Word to which he bears witness.

The Word was in the beginning, but John came. The Word is God, but John is a man. The Word is with God, but John is sent from God as a servant. The Word is the light of men, but John comes to testify concerning the light. People believe in the Word, but they believe through John. The fourth gospel is not content, the way Mark 1:7 is, to describe Jesus as more powerful than John the Baptist. Instead it draws a qualitative distinction between John and Jesus: "He who comes after me has surpassed me because he was before me" (1:15). Though historically Jesus comes after John, Jesus is before all things, for he is the Word.

John's Advent Message

"What is John the Baptist's Advent message? First, take a fresh look at the covenant Christ cut with you in his blood, your Christian commitment to mirror Christ day in and day out, and then repent: Reform your life, change your thinking, excise whatever is less than Christ-like in you. Second, recognize with St. Paul that 'now we see in a mirror dimly' (1 Cor. 13:12), realize that the face of Christ is not easy to discern, and then redouble your struggle to discover him—in the Word proclaimed and the Bread broken, in your God-filled heart and the empty eyes of the crucified all around you. Third, focus on the fact that God-in-flesh lies no longer in straw but in you, let this realization suffuse not your intellect alone but your whole being, and then let go—let the joy that *is* Christ thrill you beyond your power to control."

—Walter J. Burghardt, *Still Proclaiming Your Wonders,* New York: Paulist Press, 1985, p. 24.

The fourth gospel pictures John exclusively as a witness to Christ (John 1:7). John has no other function. He is not the forerunner of Jesus, for the Word was already before John (1:15, 30) and therefore can have no forerunners. In the fourth gospel John disowns all titles people try to give him. When religious leaders ask John who he is, John answers that he is not the Messiah, or Elijah, or the Prophet (1:19-21). Pressed for an answer, John says he is merely the voice of one calling in the desert, "Make straight the way of the Lord" (Isa. 40:3). John is the ideal witness to Christ whose one goal is self-effacement before Christ: "He must become greater; I must become less" (John 3:30). Several passages in the fourth gospel illustrate how John became "less":

- Jesus is the Lamb of God who takes away the sin of the world (1:29). But if Jesus takes away the sin of the world, then John's baptism can no longer be for the forgiveness of sins. John's sole reason for baptizing is that Jesus "might be revealed to Israel" (1:31).
- Jesus baptizes with the Holy Spirit; John with water (1:33).
- Jesus "baptizes" more people than John (4:1-2).
- Jesus is the bridegroom; John, his friend (3:29).
- Jesus comes from above; John is from the earth (3:31).
- John's witness is that of a human and is unnecessary (5:34, 36).
- John never performed a miraculous sign (10:41).

Summary

Each of the four gospels looks at John from a different angle. Mark presents John as Elijah incognito, just as he presents Jesus as the Messiah incognito. Matthew openly states that John is the Elijah who is to come and develops his role in terms of the kingdom. Luke avoids John's identification as Elijah and offers an elaborate comparison between John and Jesus that firmly establishes John's subordinate role. And Luke, more than the other gospels, places John on the world stage. Finally, the fourth gospel portrays John as someone whose one and only goal is self-effacement before Christ: "He must become greater; I must become less" (3:30).

BRINGING THE KINGDOM

J esus' coming into the world was not a visit; it was an invasion. Jesus
invades territory occupied by Caesar Augustus and King Herod. He
not only proclaims God's rule; he actually inaugurates it. He calls this
rule "the kingdom of God." Everything Jesus says and does centers on that
kingdom. The word *kingdom* sums up Jesus' entire ministry.

In the first three gospels, the term *kingdom of God* or *kingdom of heaven*
appears about a hundred times. In the gospel of John it only appears twice
(3:3, 5). John substitutes the language of life for the language of the kingdom. If the first three gospels sum up Jesus' ministry with the term kingdom, John does it with the term *life* or *eternal life*. In John, Jesus is the life
(11:25; 14:6). He calls himself "the bread of life" (6:35, 48). All the words he
speaks are life (6:63). His mission is to impart life. The reason he came is that
everyone "may have life, and have it to the full" (10:10). Life, like kingdom,
is a present reality. It is something to be had here and now.

In this chapter we will explore what the first three gospels teach about
the kingdom. We will find that they speak with such a degree of unanimity
that pursuing differences between them is rather unprofitable. Though this
book deals with the differences among the gospels, it would be strange to
not take time out to reflect on what the gospels have in common. Each

gospel presents a different variation on a common theme. In the first three gospels this common theme is called "the kingdom of God."

What Is the Kingdom?

What is that kingdom? What does it stand for? The kingdom of God, as Jesus uses the term, is not something different from our world. It is not some realm in the sky where people hope to go after they die. Matthew's use of the term *kingdom of heaven* may lead us to think that Jesus is talking about the kingdom *in* heaven rather than *of* heaven, but nothing is farther from the truth. Matthew, out of reverence for God's name, simply prefers to use the word *heaven*. So when Jesus uses the terms *kingdom of God* and *kingdom of heaven* in the gospels, he is talking about God's rule already beginning on this earth.

What is the kingdom of God? It is what life on earth would be like if God were King. It is our world as God envisions it and as God is making it. It is life lived in God's way. It is, in Robert Funk's words, "an alternate construal of reality." It is another reality already present in the everyday world. To be aware of it, we must learn to see from two perspectives at once. In addition to seeing the world we live in—the world of our senses, the world of business and politics—we must see the world as God envisions it, the world where business and politics are done God's way. Jesus' ministry brings these two worlds together.

The kingdom of God that Jesus ushers in is not something static. It is not a place or community ruled by God. No, this kingdom is dynamic. It is every act of God that reveals God's kingly rule. The parallel lines in Psalm 145:11-12 clarify this:

> They will tell of the glory of your kingdom
> and speak of your might,
> so that all men may know of your mighty acts
> and the glorious splendor of your kingdom.

The kingdom of God, the psalmist says, is expressed in God's mighty acts. For God's mighty acts reveal that God is king. The kingdom of God means God ruling as king.

The ruling power of God, still to be fully established, will mean that God's name is hallowed, his will is done on earth, all people are properly fed, all sins are forgiven, and all evil is overcome. Christians are still praying for this kind of kingdom. In this world God may already rule *de jure* (by right), but he does not yet rule *de facto* (completely). His rule still faces stiff opposition. Nevertheless, the kingdom of God will fully come—but only after God has destroyed "the last enemy," death.

Kingdom Language

How does Jesus speak about the kingdom of God in the first three gospels? What language does he use? How does he describe the invisible rule of God to people who can't see what he's talking about?

Jesus mostly uses metaphors when he talks about the kingdom of God. A metaphor is a figure of speech that sees one thing as something else. A metaphor equates something unfamiliar with something familiar. Jesus' metaphors tell us about the unfamiliar kingdom of God through familiar scenes of everyday life. The kingdom of God, Jesus says, is like a mustard seed planted in a field, or like yeast mixed into a large amount of flower, or like a net let down into a lake that catches a lot of fish, or like seed springing up, or like a man preparing a great banquet and inviting many guests. (Some of the metaphors Jesus uses are actually short stories; we call these story-like metaphors "parables." The next session will explore some of these in detail.) Jesus uses many metaphors to paint pictures of the kingdom of God, but he does not explicitly define what this kingdom is.

Jesus' pictures bring the kingdom to life. Still, we wonder, why does Jesus use metaphorical language? Why doesn't he come right out and tell us in straight and unambiguous language what the kingdom is? One answer is that we find it hard to absorb unfamiliar truth directly. We can only begin to learn about the invisible kingdom of God indirectly, with the help of metaphors that describe that unfamiliar kingdom in terms of scenes that are

The Kingdom Is a Public Park

"What is the Kingdom of God, according to the prophet Zechariah? It is a public park. It is a park where old people are no longer cold and lonely and ill and senile, but participants in a community. It is a public park where the elderly can sit together and bask in the sun, and talk and laugh over the good old days in full vigor and clear mind and satisfaction of life.

"The Kingdom of God is a public park where little children can run and play in its squares, in safety and fun and delight. It is a place where no pervert is waiting to lure one of them away with offers of candy; where no drug pusher is lurking to tempt the older children to try a brightly colored pill. It is a place where no child is abused or unwanted or malnourished, and where there is not even a bully among the group, shoving and taunting the littler ones until they break into tears. The Kingdom of God, says Zechariah, is a public park where the streets are safe for children."

—Elizabeth Achtemeier, *Best Sermons 1*, ed. James W. Cox and Kenneth M. Cox, San Francisco: Harper & Row, 1988, p. 288ff.

What Is the Kingdom of God?

"What is the kingdom of God? [Jesus] speaks of what it is like to find a diamond ring that you thought you'd lost forever. He speaks of what it is like to win the Irish Sweepstakes. He suggests rather than spells out. He evokes rather than explains. He catches by surprise. He doesn't let the homiletic seams show. He is sometimes cryptic, sometimes obscure, sometimes irreverent, always provocative."

—Frederick Buechner, *Telling the Truth*, New York: Harper & Row, 1977, p. 62ff.

familiar to us. This explains why Jesus' language so frequently is nonliteral. In literal language growing seed is growing seed. In Jesus' metaphorical language growing seed is the growing rule of God. In literal language mixing yeast and flour is part of the process of baking bread. In Jesus' metaphorical language mixing yeast into flour is God's kingly rule penetrating all human relations.

When it comes to metaphors, children have a decided advantage over adults. To whom does the kingdom of God belong? Jesus' answer is unexpected: "Let the children come to me, and do not hinder them, for the kingdom of God belongs to such as these. I tell you the truth, anyone who will not receive the kingdom of God like a child will never enter it" (Mark 10:14-15; Matt. 19:14; Luke 18:16).

What does Jesus see in children that make them our models? What qualities of children do adults need to receive the kingdom? Is it children's innocence and purity? Perhaps, but children can be mean and cruel; children can steal and lie. There's something else. Some of the meaning of Jesus' saying dawns on us when we recall how differently from adults children see things. Children, more easily than adults, are able to see with the eye of imagination. They wander more easily into imaginary worlds, the world of fairy tales, for example. They therefore wander more easily into the world of the kingdom of God, too. They have a greater capacity to see the magic and wonder of things like, "Ask and it will be given to you; seek and you will find; knock and the door will be opened to you" (Matt. 7:7; Luke 11:9). But what often happens as the child grows into an adult? The mind narrows, vision shortens, and the eyes of imagination grow dim. What is hidden from the wise and learned, God reveals to little children (Matt. 11:25; Luke 10:21). Though they do not know it, children have an easier time seeing God's world in this world.

The Kingdom and Repentance

Jesus says that in order to enter the kingdom of God we must repent. In his inaugural speech he says, "The time has come. The kingdom of God is near. Repent and believe the good news!" (Mark 1:15; cf. Matt. 4:17). Entrance into the kingdom requires an act of repentance. What does Jesus mean by repentance? For the answer let's first listen to John the Baptist. John tells the Israelites of his day that if they do not produce fruit in keeping with repentance, God will raise up children for Abraham out of stones (Matt. 3:9; Luke 3:8). In other words, to have "children of Abraham" God does not have to depend on people who are physically descended from Abraham. But to fulfill his promise to Abraham that "all peoples on earth shall be blessed through you" (Gen. 12:3), God needs a people, a people relating to Abraham on a spiritual level, a people producing fruit in keeping with repentance. So the repentance John preaches is not only a call for each sinner to repent. John isn't only demanding a moral turning from private sin. He wants nothing less than nationwide repentance.

Jesus' call for repentance is similar. Jesus "came to that which was his own, but his own did not receive him" (John 1:11). Jesus summons the Israel of his day to abandon its own agenda and embrace God's agenda. Jesus, says N. T. Wright, is not first of all calling for an individual moral repentance. That kind of *ad hoc* repentance could be done at any time in Israel and, of itself, would not indicate the end-time coming of the kingdom of God. "Jesus' summons was more radical by far. . . . Jesus was urging his compatriots to abandon a whole way of life, and to trust him for a different one" (*Jesus and the Victory of God,* p. 258). Jesus wants the Jews to follow him into a different way of being Israel.

The Kingdom Is Hidden

If God's kingdom is near, where is it? If God's kingdom has arrived, where can we see it? Here we run into a problem—for the kingdom is hidden from us. It is hidden in the everyday world of the present time, and no one is aware of what is taking place. For the time being the kingdom advances out of view. The new age *has* come, but the old age remains until the new completely overcomes the old.

The kingdom of God, Jesus says, is "like yeast that a woman took and mixed into a large amount of flour until it worked all through the dough" (Matt. 13:33; Luke 13:21). Concealed from the human eye, the yeast permeates the whole lump, changing the shape and texture of the dough completely. At first nothing appears to happen. Then, gradually, the dough begins to swell and bubble. The kingdom of God is like that. It is like the entire leavening process. It is the hidden power of God transforming the entire lump of humanity.

Again, says Jesus, the kingdom of God "is like a mustard seed, which is the smallest seed you plant in the ground. Yet when planted, it grows and becomes the largest of all garden plants, with such big branches that the birds of the air can perch in its shade" (Mark 4:31-32; cf. Matt. 13:31-32; Luke 13:18-19). God's kingdom is hidden in the small and insignificant. The greatest things are hidden in the smallest things. Magnificent things are hidden in insignificant things.

Or observe the behavior of a farmer. He "scatters seed on the ground. Night and day, whether he sleeps or gets up, the seed sprouts and grows, though he does not know how. All by itself the soil produces grain—first the stalk, then the head, then the full kernel in the head. As soon as the grain is ripe, he puts the sickle to it, because the harvest has come" (Mark 4:26-29). God is like that farmer. Even though God is working all the time, the grain grows in a hidden way. God may seem passive and unconcerned, like the farmer who gets up and goes to bed. But in the fullness of time, God will show his rule for all to see.

The prime example of the hidden nature of God's kingdom, however, is Jesus himself. He, after all, embodies the kingdom of God. Jesus' life as a whole, including his death and resurrection, proclaims the kingly rule of God. The life story of Jesus discloses a new way of living in the world, a way marked by total submission to the rule of God. But somehow no one sees the kingdom of God in Jesus. Somehow everyone misses it. "He was in the world," writes John, "and though the world was made through him, the world did not recognize him" (1:10). And, as we saw in chapter 1, the hiddenness of Jesus' identity is the big point Mark makes in his gospel. The crowds, the scribes, the high priest, the disciples, and Jesus' family—they all wonder who Jesus is. And they all miss seeing the kingdom of God in the life of Jesus. That Jesus embodies the kingdom is hidden from their eyes.

No Distant Vision

"Whereas the apocalyptic seers spoke of events and things which were outside themselves, Jesus brings the kingdom along with him. For him, it is no distant vision. He is at the very centre, involved in a battle with another kingdom. . . . But there is nothing world-shattering to be seen. . . . There is no national uprising, there are no signs in the heavens, but only something of God and heaven which is hidden in daily life, in the workaday world of man."

—*A New Catechism*, New York: Herder and Herder, 1967, p. 96ff.

The Kingdom Has Arrived

Jesus proclaims that the kingdom of God has arrived with him. The proof, Jesus says, is his ability to cast out demons. When Jewish leaders accuse him of being in league with the prince of demons, of casting out demons by the power of Beelzebub, Jesus replies that his exorcisms are actually evidences that the kingdom of God has arrived: "But if I drive out demons by the finger of God, then the kingdom of God has come to you" (Luke 11:20; cf. Matt. 12:28). The words "the finger of God" recall the story of the Egyptian magicians who were incapable of duplicating Moses' act of turning dust into gnats. In the plague of gnats the Egyptians saw the superior power of Israel's God (Ex. 8:19). Jesus is modeling his answer to the Jewish leaders after this story. It would be absurd for the prince of demons, he is saying, to supply the power necessary to cast out demons. The world of demons would only be destroying itself. So the only other possible source of power is the God of Israel who once used his power to liberate his people from Egyptian slavery and who is now, through Jesus, exerting that same power to set his people free from demonic power. Jesus' exorcisms are battles with the evil one: "Every occasion on which Jesus drives out an evil spirit is an anticipation of the hour in which Satan will be visibly robbed of his power. The victories over his instruments are a foretaste of the eschaton" (Joachim Jeremias, *New Testament Theology*, p. 95).

Matthew and Luke reinforce the idea that the kingdom of God arrives with Jesus by reporting that John the Baptist sent disciples to Jesus with the question, "Are you the one who was to come, or should we expect someone else?" (Matt. 11:3; Luke 7:19). Jesus answers this question indirectly by pointing to the public record of his ministry, letting John draw the conclusion for himself. Report what you hear and see, he says: "The blind receive sight, the lame walk, those who have leprosy are cured, the deaf hear, the dead are raised, and the good news is preached to the poor." Jesus' reply signals a shift in message from John's emphasis on the God who judges those who do not repent. Jesus instead speaks of the God who comes in power and mercy to heal and redeem his people. Even though these passages in Matthew and Luke do not use the phrase "kingdom of God," they supply the background for understand-

> **Why I'm a Pastor**
>
> "I believe that the kingdoms of this world, American and Venezuelan and Chinese, will become the kingdom of our God and Christ, and I believe this new kingdom is already among us. That is why I'm a pastor, to introduce people to the real world and train them to live in it."
>
> —Eugene H. Peterson, *The Contemplative Pastor*, Carol Stream, Ill.: Word Publishing, 1989, p. 38.

ing the phrase when it does appear a couple of verses later. In Matthew and Luke, Jesus stands in contrast to John the Baptist as one who does miracles of healing and proclaims good news to the poor. This is how God's kingly rule operates in the end-time. It operates through the healing and preaching ministry of Jesus.

The Kingdom and Forgiveness

With the arrival of the kingdom comes the forgiveness of sins. When the birth of Jesus is announced, the name given him is interpreted as "he will save his people from their sins" (Matt. 1:21). The forgiveness of sins is at the center of Jesus' gospel of the kingdom of God.

The Jews of Jesus' day had a highly developed sense of sin and an elaborate system for dealing with it. Any transgression of the law of God was sin. And sin put a person in debt to God. This debt could be paid in a variety of ways, but none of them was sufficient to secure forgiveness. The important thing in the Jewish notion of fulfilling the law of God, writes Herman Ridderbos, "is that the number of infringements of the law should be inferior to the number of fulfillments of the law. In other words, the credit side of man's account with God must be greater than his debit side. . . . There is, however, no certainty of salvation for the righteous" (*The Coming of the Kingdom,* p. 218).

First century Judaism recognized three classes of sinners: Jewish sinners who turned to God in penitence and hope; Gentile sinners, whom most Jews regarded as beyond the reach of God's mercy; and Jewish sinners who had made themselves as Gentiles. The last group is often referred to in the gospels as "sinners"; these sinners were widely regarded as being beyond forgiveness.

It is against this background that we must hear Jesus proclaim the forgiveness of sins. Jesus breaks with the entire Jewish scheme of forgiveness. Jesus brings the message of forgiveness in words, in pictures, and in actions.

In Direct Words

One day Jesus tells a paralytic who has come to him for healing, "Son, your sins are forgiven" (Mark 2:1-12; cf. Matt. 9:1-8; Luke 5:17-26). Some theological experts who hear this think to themselves, "He's blaspheming! Who can forgive sins but God alone?" While they are fuming, Jesus drops this loaded question: "Which is easier: to say to the paralytic, 'Your sins are forgiven,' or to say, 'Get up, take your mat and walk'?"

Obviously, it's much easier to say "your sins are forgiven" than to make a lame man walk again. But to show that he has authority on earth to forgive sins, Jesus says, "Get up." The new and unprecedented thing here is not that Jesus announces the forgiveness of sins but that he actually effects it. The power to forgive sins on earth is the power Jesus possesses as the one who embodies the kingdom of God. God, whose kingdom he brings, authorizes Jesus to deliver people from their sins here and now.

In Pictures

Jesus most often proclaimed the forgiveness of sins by sketching word pictures. In Matthew, for example, Jesus pictures the God who forgives sins as a king who takes pity on one of his servants who owes him several million dollars (18:21-35). In Luke, Jesus describes God as a moneylender who cancels a big and a small debt (7:41-43). Another time Jesus tells a story of a tax collector who prayed, "God, have mercy on me, a sinner," and went home justified before God (18:13). Still another time, to Jewish leaders who accuse him of eating with sinners, Jesus tells the story of the shepherd who leaves the ninety-nine and goes after the lost sheep until he finds it (15:1-7). Also in Luke, Jesus tells the story of the father who runs to meet his returning son, putting on him the best robe, a ring on his finger and sandals on his feet—all marks of a free man (15:1-32).

In Actions

Jesus also proclaims forgiveness of sins through actions. For example, Jesus eats with tax collectors and "sinners," people considered to be ritually or morally unclean. Breaking bread with these people is an offensive act to Jesus' critics. When they see Jesus reclining at table with tax collectors and "sinners," they denounce him as "a glutton and a drunkard, a friend of tax collectors and 'sinners'" (Matt. 11:19). To grasp what Jesus is doing, it is essential to realize that in the Middle East to invite a man to a meal means offering him trust and peace and forgiveness. In Judaism, Joachim Jeremias writes, "table-fellowship means fellowship before God, for the eating of a piece of broken bread by everyone who shares in the meal brings out the fact that they all have a share in the blessing which the master of the house had spoken over the unbroken bread" (*New Testament Theology,* p. 115). By eating with tax collectors and "sinners," Jesus is celebrating God's merciful embracing of his prodigal children. His banquets with sinful Israelites are celebrations anticipating the messianic banquet at the end of time when "many will come from the east and the west, and will take their places at the feast with Abraham, Isaac and Jacob in the kingdom of heaven" (Matt. 8:11). By attending these banquets, Jesus is powerfully proclaiming the forgiveness of sins.

The Constitution of the Kingdom

When the kingdom of God arrives with Jesus, as we've seen, Jesus casts out demons, heals the sick, eats with tax collectors and "sinners," and forgives sins. Jesus dispenses undeserved grace. But with this grace comes a demand. Those who have received grace are called to show grace. God's forgiveness of our sins demands that we forgive those who sin against us (Mark 11:25; Matt. 6:14-15). And God's impartial love that causes his sun to rise on the evil and the good demands that we love not only those who love us but also those who hate us (Matt. 5:43-48; Luke 6:27-28, 32-26). Jesus demands that those who have received grace reciprocate by showing grace to others.

Many of Jesus' demands are found in the Sermon on the Mount (Matt. 5-7), partly paralleled by the Sermon on the Plain (Luke 6:20-49). The Sermon on the Mount has been called the constitution of the kingdom of God. It is not a code of behavior to be obeyed legalistically. Rather, it describes the behavior of a community that lives by the grace of God manifested in the ministry of Jesus. Who belongs to this community? The people whom Jesus calls blessed at the beginning of the sermon: the poor in spirit, those who mourn, the meek, those who hunger and thirst for righteousness, the merciful, the pure in heart, the peacemakers, the persecuted. Theirs is the kingdom of God. For them the future that God promised in the Old Testament has begun to be present. One theologian points out that Jesus calls these people the light of the world, "not primarily because of what they *do,* but what they *receive.* But that light must beam forth, for men do not light a lamp and put it under a bushel. What Jesus thus requires is that men reflect the light which they received from Him" (Herman Ridderbos, *When the Time Has Fully Come,* Grand Rapids, Mich.: Eerdmans Publishing Co., 1957, p. 31).

The Sermon on the Mount is not what we often take it to be. It is not a grand moral code that nobody is able to live here and now. It is not morality for a future time, when the rule of God has been fully established. No, the Sermon on the Mount spells out kingdom behavior in this life and in this world. But it does so in terms of the total gospel story. This means that the Sermon on the Mount makes sense only from the perspective of Jesus' resurrection—for without Jesus' resurrection there is no gospel. If Jesus has not been raised, all his teaching is useless. That's why Jesus never allowed his disciples to focus his ministry exclusively in his teaching. The ultimate focus of Jesus' ministry is his resurrection. Faith in Jesus' resurrection controls not only the Sermon on the Mount; it controls everything the gospels say. The gospels do not just end with Jesus' resurrection; they also begin with it. Everything written in the gospels is written from the conviction that Jesus rose from the dead. Without that conviction, there would be no gospel and no Sermon on the Mount. This sermon only makes sense to those who read it from the perspective of Easter. The morality of this sermon is Easter morality. It is morality propelled by Jesus' resurrection power. And that "great power" as Paul reminds us in a different context (Eph. 2:19-20)—power to live the kingdom way—is available to those who believe.

SESSION 5

TELLING PARABLES

J esus teaches in parables. In fact, parables are Jesus' favorite teaching device. This is true, at least, of the first three gospels, in which Jesus uses parables when he talks about the kingdom of God. But in the gospel of John, except for two occurrences, the term "kingdom of God" is altogether missing. In John, Jesus talks of himself rather than of the kingdom of God. Here the parables of the kingdom seem to make a place for figurative speech centered on the person of Jesus. If in the first three gospels the kingdom is like yeast working in a mass of dough, in the fourth gospel Jesus is the bread of life. If in the earlier gospels there is a parable of the shepherd and the lost sheep, in the gospel of John Jesus is the good shepherd.

What Are Parables?

When we turn to Jesus' parables of the kingdom in the first three gospels, our first question is, What are parables? In the history of the church this question has been answered in a variety of ways:

1. *Parables are earthly stories with a heavenly meaning.* If this definition means that Jesus tells parables to focus our minds on heavenly things, then it is forcing parables to act against their own interior design.

Parables don't point to a heavenly world beyond this world; they point to a new possibility in this world. Rather than turn us away from our current life and toward life after death, parables seek to open our eyes to the presence of God's kingdom right in the world of our everyday experiences. That's why Jesus' parables created such a stir. That's why they landed Jesus in trouble. William R. Herzog puts it this way: "If Jesus was a teacher of heavenly truths dispensed through literary gems called parables, it is difficult to understand how he could have been executed as a political subversive and crucified between two social bandits" (*Parables as Subversive Speech,* Louisville: Westminster/John Knox Press, 1994, p. 9).

2. *Parables are illustrations.* In this view parables are stories that illustrate a difficult moral or theological point. This interpretation makes the form—a story—of marginal importance. For can't a moral or theological point be made just as well by other, less dramatic, means? Jesus' parables are not illustrations used to illumine a basic idea.

3. *Parables are allegories.* From the beginning of the Christian era, Jesus' parables have been widely treated as allegories—encoded stories that veil their message in secrecy. In an allegory everything equals something else. When the parable of ten virgins (Matt. 25:1-13), for example, is read as an allegory, the bridegroom equals Jesus, the bridegroom's delay equals the delay of Jesus' second coming, the wedding equals the kingdom of God, the shut door equals the last judgment, the wise virgins equal the true believers, and the foolish virgins equal the backsliders.

    There are two dangers in reading parables as allegories. First, explanations offered tend to be arbitrary. Those who allegorize often use parables as pegs on which to hang their theological wardrobe. Second, once the "coded" parable has been translated into a text readily understood, the parable itself tends to be set aside. But Jesus' parables can never be dispensed with, for they express what cannot be expressed any better way. Each translation of a parable always says less than the parable itself.

    We must not, however, reject allegorizing as such, for Jesus engaged in it too, though only on rare occasions and only in the disciples' presence. In three of the parables that Jesus allegorized—the parable of the sower (Mark 4:13-20 and parallels), the parable of the weeds (Matt. 13:36-43), and the parable of the net (Matt. 13:49-50)—Jesus explained the details of his stories. As we will see later on in this chapter, Matthew and Luke also did some allegorizing.

4. *Parables are one-point stories*. This view first became popular after the 1886 publication of Adolf Juelicher's book on the parables of Jesus. According to Juelicher, every parable has just one central point. The details of the parable have no independent meaning of their own, the way they do in allegories; instead they serve only to enhance that one point. The meaning of a parable, Juelicher is saying, is like a drop of oil floating in a cup of water. Once the oil drop has been retrieved, we can throw away the water. Once the central meaning of the parable has been extracted, the parable story itself serves no further purpose.

The fallacy of this theory is that the meaning of a parable resists being reduced to a single point that, like a drop of oil, floats on the surface of the story. The parable's meaning, rather, is dispersed throughout the entire story. As theologian Walter Wink says, "Juelicher merely substituted for an allegorizing of the parts an allegorizing of the whole. In this he has been followed by almost every commentator until recent times. The reduction of every parable to a single point (read: *idea*) renders it a mere illustration of more primary theological meanings. Lost is all sense of the parable's artistic integrity, its capacity to tell us something we do not know and could not come by in any other way, its ability to evoke experiences we have never had, and an awareness of realities we have not even guessed at before" (*The Christian Century*, November 5, 1980, p. 1063).

Parable as Metaphor

If Walter Wink is right, if the valid interpretation of Jesus' parables is a multi-dimensional experience, then recent parable studies viewing parables primarily as story metaphors have much to commend themselves. Today, in a break with Juelicher, many biblical scholars view parables as metaphors. A metaphor sees one thing as something else; it says that A is B. It says, for example, that "all people *are* grass," the Lord *is* my shepherd, Jesus *is* a vine. A metaphor equates the unknown A with the known B, the unfamiliar A with the familiar B. By

Parables Jolt

"The parables shock the mind into opening to the unenvisioned possible; they madly exaggerate in order to jolt the consciousness of the religiously secure; they are an assault upon the obvious. The entire momentum of conventional piety is brought into question: the man sells everything for the one thing; the shepherd leaves the 99 undefended in order to find the lost one; in defiance of common sense, the woman takes the house apart to find the lost coin; the lord commends the unjust steward for his uncanny perception of the truth."

—Joseph Sittler, *Gravity and Grace*, Minneapolis: Augsburg Publishing House, 1986, p. 110.

equating two things that are usually not equated, by equating what is unknown to what is known, a metaphor reveals something new. It offers a fresh, unique insight that takes us by surprise. Jesus uses this type of metaphorical equation in his parables.

The Parable of the Mustard Seed
(Mark 4:30-32; Matt. 13:31-32; Luke 13:18-19)

Jesus says the kingdom of God is "a mustard seed, which is the smallest seed you plant in the ground. Yet when planted, it grows and becomes the largest of all garden plants, with such big branches that the birds of the air can perch in its shade" (Mark 4:30-32). Take note: Jesus does not just equate the kingdom with a mustard seed. The whole story, not just the seed, illumines what the kingdom is. In Mark's version, this parable is one of *contrast*. The mustard seed is "the smallest seed you plant in the ground." Yet when it grows it becomes "the largest of all garden plants." Mark's parable creates a contrast between small beginnings and great results. The smallness of the mustard seed was proverbial in Jesus' day. We know this, for example, from a saying like Matthew 17:20: "[I]f you have faith as small as a mustard seed, you can say to this mountain, 'Move from here to there' and it will move." The smallest thing, Jesus is saying, can move the largest thing. Both Matthew and Luke (but not Mark) say that the mustard seed becomes a tree. But the mustard plant is actually an annual that normally grows to four feet, although at times to eight or even ten feet. Why do the two writers then call it a tree? Most likely to recall those Old Testament passages in which a tall tree sheltering birds symbolizes an empire offering political protection to its subject states. In Ezekiel 31:2-6, for example, the power of Pharaoh's empire and its subject states is compared to a mighty cedar in Lebanon with all the birds of the air nesting in its boughs. In Daniel 4:10-12, Nebuchadnezzar's Babylonian Empire is compared to a tree so large that its top touched the sky while "the birds of the air lived in its branches." And in Ezekiel 17:22-23 the image of the Lebanese cedar is used again—this time to symbolize the Messiah. Ezekiel is describing the messianic kingdom when he says, "Birds of every kind will nest in it; they will find shelter in the shade of its branches." So in the Old Testament, the great cedar of Lebanon with birds in its branches was considered a fitting image not only for the mighty kingdoms of Babylon and Egypt but also for the messianic kingdom. In comparison to this mighty cedar, the mustard plant is a pitiful specimen. Jesus chooses a humble image, "one which is a deliberate lampoon on the cedar's pretentiousness. The kingdom of God is *not* like the proverbial cedar of Lebanon but is like the very ordinary mustard plant. This is a satiric thrust at the earlier image with its apocalyptic tree whose 'top reached to heaven' in Daniel 4:11, the tree with its 'top among the clouds' in Ezekiel 31:3" (John Dominic Crossan, *The Dark Interval,* p. 95).

Mark's and Matthew's version of the parable of the mustard seed are quite similar, but Luke's is not. Luke makes no sharp contrast between the smallest and the greatest. Luke might just as well have used the image of any other seed. In fact, Herman Hendricks points out, "any other seed would have done better in his version, because the mustard seed does not develop into a tree, as his source said, but only into a bush or shrub, as Mark correctly says" (*The Parables of Jesus,* San Francisco: Harper & Row, 1986, p. 33). But Luke, ignoring the contrast between smallness and greatness, simply focuses his attention on growth. The seed grows and becomes a tree. Luke's treatment of this parable is consistent with his perspective throughout his two-volume work, Luke and Acts. Luke's purpose is to trace the growth of Christianity from a sect of Judaism into a world religion.

Jesus Subverts Conventional Wisdom

A parable typically begins in the familiar everyday world with its conventional standards and expectations. Then in the course of the story a radically different perspective appears that disorients the listeners. Finally, the conventional and the new perspective interact to create tension, resulting in a redescription of life in the world. A parable, in other words, is an assault on the conventional way of viewing the world. It seeks to break the grip of tradition on our understanding of the world in order to allow us a glimpse of God's world. A parable, writes Sallie McFague, "is an assault on the social, economic, and mythic structures people build for their own comfort and security. A parable is a story meant to invert and subvert these structures and to suggest that the way of the kingdom is not the way of the world" (*Metaphorical Theology,* Philadelphia: Fortress, 1982, p. 47).

Parables Shatter the Status Quo

"They are stories which shatter the deep structure of our accepted world and therefore render clear and evident to us the relativity of story itself. They remove our defenses and make us vulnerable to God. It is only in such experiences that God can touch us, and only in such moments does the kingdom of God arrive."

—John Dominic Crossan, *The Dark Interval,* p. 122.

Parables Reveal a New World

"The parables of Jesus help us to see two realities: the reality of a world whose values must be rejected, and the reality of a new world whose values must be accepted. It is easy for us to live in a comfortable culture and to assimilate the values of a kingdom of God into a system produced, so the historians tell us, by our Judeo-Christian heritage. The American Jesus comes to us rather tamely, tidies up a few bad habits, makes us better citizens, and sends us back into a 'civilization' that is grateful for our good influence. Everything flows smoothly. Christianity seems warm and right to us. There is no comprehensive discontinuity between what we have been and what we are or shall be. There is no rejection of traditional values, and, sadly, there is no entrance into the kingdom of God."

—Clarence Jordan and Bill Lane Doulos, *Cotton Patch Parables of Liberation,* Scottdale, Penn.: Herald Press, 1976, p. 17.

Parables destroy the wisdom of the wise and frustrate the intelligence of the intelligent. By equating God's unfamiliar kingdom with familiar human scenes, Jesus confounds our wisdom with God's foolishness and challenges everything we thought we knew for sure. Conventional wisdom praises us for building ourselves a beautiful home. Then Jesus' parable whispers in our ear, "You fool! You built it right above an earthquake fault." Conventional wisdom praises us for making wise investments. Then Jesus' parable whispers in our ear, "You fool! This very night your life will be demanded from you. Who then will prosper from your investments?" In Jesus' parables a man sells everything to obtain one thing; a shepherd leaves the ninety-nine sheep in order to find the lost one; a lord commends his shrewd manager for making a realistic assessment of the crisis he is in. What these people do jolts us and catches us off guard. We are unsettled even more by late-arriving workers being paid the same as early-arriving workers; an extravagant banquet given for the poor and marginalized when the prominent decline to come; a despised Samaritan coming to the aid of a Jewish traveler while upstanding religious folk walk on by. In each of these stories conventional wisdom is subverted by a new wisdom—that of the kingdom of God.

Conventional wisdom, Marcus J. Borg writes, "is the dominant consciousness of any culture. It is a culture's most taken-for-granted understanding about the way things are (its worldview, or image of reality) and about the way to live (its ethos, or way of life). It is 'what everybody knows'—the world that everybody is socialized into through the process of growing up. It is a culture's social construction of reality and the internalization of that construction within the psyche of the individual" (*Meeting Jesus Again for the First Time,* p. 75).

To each culture, conventional wisdom provides three basic services: first, it provides concrete guidance about how to live; second, it orders life on the basis of rewards and punishments; and third, it creates a world of boundaries—those of gender, race, and social class. In short, conventional wisdom creates the world we live in. Life in this world is a life under the lordship of the dominant culture. We see what our culture conditions us to see. We say what our culture conditions us to say.

Central to the conventional wisdom of Jesus' day was the idea of holiness. This core value was based on Leviticus 19:2: "Be holy because I, the Lord your God, am holy." Here Israel is called to imitate God; because God is holy, Israel is to be holy. This is to be Israel's way of life.

So far so good. But how is holiness understood? In Jesus' day holiness was understood as separation—separation from external sources of defilement. That is, holiness was understood as purity, and purity had become the conventional wisdom around which first-century Jewish society was structured. Society was organized around the contrast of pure and impure. This pure-impure contrast was projected onto other contrasts such as rich and poor, healthy and sick, male and female, Jew and Gentile. So in conventional wisdom, health testified to purity; sickness to impurity. Also, wealth made pure, extreme poverty made impure; wealth was a blessing from God, but poverty was evidence of not living right. And because childbirth and menstruation were seen as sources of impurity, men were generally thought to be more pure than women. Finally, the pure-impure contrast was applied to the Jew-Gentile contrast. Being Jewish did not of itself guarantee purity, but being a Gentile automatically made one impure. In short, the pure-impure contrast created a world with sharp social boundaries.

In a number of parables, Jesus attacks this purity system at the heart of Jewish society. Take, for example, the well-known parable of the Good Samaritan (Luke 10:25-37). What makes the priest and the Levite pass by the man beaten by robbers? Conventional wisdom, the holiness program of the Pharisees, the responsibility of priests and Levites to enforce holiness regulations. If the person on the side of the road is a Gentile or is already dead, touching him will lead to being ritually defiled. On the other hand, if he is a Jew, the priest and Levite have an obligation to help. But it takes a close look to properly identify the person—and that creates the risk of being defiled. Of course, if a person were defiled there were provisions for purification, but these were costly and time-consuming. In short, the parable of the Good Samaritan is an attack on the holiness ideal operating at the core of Jewish society. The behavior of the priest and Levite, Jesus is saying, though consistent with the holiness model, really amounts to the failure to be a neighbor.

The Parable of the Great Banquet
(Matt. 22:1-14; Luke 14:16-24)

In Luke's version of this parable, Jesus is the guest of a prominent Pharisee. The parable exposes the basic conflict between Jesus' and the host's vision of what Israel ought to be. The Pharisees, who virtually equate holiness with purity, believe that table fellowship and the state of purity in which the meals are eaten embody the vision of what Israel is to be. Jesus refutes the equation between holiness and purity. That is, Jesus denies that holiness equals a separation from rituals and food and guests that defile. Jesus' actions have made his stand clear.

- *Rituals.* Jesus and his disciples are accused of eating with ceremonially unwashed hands (Mark 7:1-2; Luke 11:37-38).
- *Food.* Jesus declares all foods clean (Mark 7:19).
- *Dinner guests.* Jesus habitually eats with tax collectors and "sinners."

It is against this background that we must read the parable of the Great Banquet. Luke's version is prefaced by Jesus' advice to his host: "When you give a luncheon or dinner, do not invite your friends, your brothers or relatives, or your rich neighbors" (14:12). For if you do, they're likely, of course, to reciprocate. Instead, Jesus advises, invite the people who cannot repay you—the poor, the crippled, the lame, and the blind. At this point one of the guests speaks up: "Blessed is the man who will eat at the feast in the kingdom of God" (14:15). The guest is referring to the great banquet at the end of time—the messianic banquet described in Isaiah 25:6-9 as a banquet to which all peoples—Jews and Gentiles alike—are invited.

In Jewish writings from the period between the Old and the New Testament, however, the vision of Isaiah 25 is dimmed, if not completely lost. For example, the apocryphal book of Enoch, written about 163 B.C., excludes Gentiles from the banquet. One of the Dead Sea Scrolls excludes not only Gentiles but also Jews who are unrighteous or have physical defects. This scroll maintains that those who are crippled in either hand or foot, lame or blind, deaf or dumb, senile or of poor eyesight will not be invited to the messianic banquet. They might offend the holy angels.

With that background, let's return to the guest who says to Jesus, "Blessed is the man who will eat at the feast in the kingdom of God." This man has just heard Jesus tell the host that he should invite people who are not able to repay in kind—the poor, the crippled, the lame, and the blind. By including the very people whom informed theological opinion excludes from the list of invited guests, Jesus cannot but upset his host. Coming to the rescue of the host by attempting to straighten out Jesus' theology, the guest tells Jesus that true blessedness will not come to the poor and the physically handicapped in this current age, but to men of religious status in the coming age. Jesus responds by telling a parable that only adds fuel to the fire. A certain man, Jesus says, was preparing a great banquet and invited many guests. The guests, however, refused to come. The host then invited "the poor, the crippled, the blind and the lame." With much room still available, he finally invited people outside the city—those on "the roads and country lanes."

Matthew too records the parable of the great banquet—but with significant differences. A comparison of both versions reveals eight differences:

In Matthew	In Luke
1. The host is a king.	1. The host is a certain man, the owner of the house.
2. The king invites people to the wedding feast of his son.	2. The man invites people to a great banquet.
3. Two groups of servants are sent out successively.	3. One servant is sent out once.
4. The reasons for the refusal are brief.	4. The reasons for the refusal are lengthy.
5. The second group of servants are treated violently, even killed. In anger the king sends his army, destroys the murderers, and burns their city.	5. The servant is not treated violently. Though the host gets angry, there is no mention of a punitive action.
6. The king sends out a third group of servants to the crossroads to invite anybody they can find, both good and bad.	6. The man sends out his servant twice, once to the streets of the city to bring in the poor, the crippled, the blind, and the lame, and next to the roads and country lanes to make people come in.
7. There is an inspection of the guests. One man is found without a wedding garment and is thrown out.	7. There is no inspection of the guests.
8. The final verse reads, "For many are invited, but few are chosen."	8. The final verse reads, "I tell you, not one of those men who were invited will get a taste of my banquet."

How can we explain these differences between Matthew and Luke? A comparison of Matthew's and Luke's versions of the parable shows, writes Joachim Jeremias, that their differences spring from an allegorizing tendency, and that Luke is more constrained in his use of allegory than Matthew. Whereas in Luke "the parable's original form has remained essentially unchanged," in Matthew the parable "has been transformed into nothing less than an allegory of the plan of salvation" (*Rediscovering the Parables*, p. 139). Matthew and Luke fit the parable into different time frames. Matthew sketches the history of salvation from the time of the Old Testament prophets to the last judgment. The first sending of servants suggests the Old Testament prophets and the rejection of their message (Matt. 22:3). The second sending of servants suggests the missionary activity and the death of the apostles and early Christian missionaries in Jerusalem (22:6). The destruction of this city in A.D. 70 by the Romans is interpreted as punishment for repeated Jewish rejection of God's invitation. The sending of servants to invite as many as they can find suggests the mission to the Gentiles (22:9-10). The inspection of the guests in Matthew 22:11 suggests the last judgment, and the darkness suggests hell.

In Luke, the parable's tie-in with salvation history is not as explicit and extensive. Compared to Matthew, Luke places more emphasis on bringing in the Gentiles. Luke's version of the parable reflects the same mission priority we find in the book of Acts: first to the Jews and God-fearers and then to the Gentiles. Luke, in other words, interprets the parable as a missionary command. Matthew applies the parable differently. He is after those who think they have God's salvation "in the bag." He is trying to say "that one can sit in the banquet hall without joining in the feast because he is sitting there 'without wedding clothes'; in other words, he is not totally there in his heart" (Eduard Schweizer, *The Good News According to Matthew*, Atlanta: John Knox Press, 1975, p. 421).

Parables have a life of their own. They can be transferred into many situations other than that of Jesus and his hearers. Their power is not dependent upon their original historical context. They can be explained in any number of ways. Their meaning can never be exhausted.

A Modern Parable

"It was very early in the morning, the streets clean and deserted, I was on my way to the station. As I compared the tower clock with my watch I realized it was much later than I had thought and that I had to hurry; the shock of this discovery made me feel uncertain of the way, I wasn't very well acquainted with the town as yet; fortunately, there was a policeman at hand, I ran to him and breathlessly asked him the way. He smiled and said, 'You are asking me the way?' 'Yes,' I said, 'Since I can't find it myself.' 'Give it up! Give it up!' said he, and turned with a sudden jerk, like someone who wants to be alone with his laughter."

—*Franz Kafka: The Complete Stories*, New York: Schocken Books, 1971, p. 456.

SESSION 6

DOING MIRACLES

What Are Miracles?

I t is quite common for Christians to assume that Jesus did miracles in order to prove that he was more than human. Jesus' miracles, Christians say, prove his divinity. From here it is only a short step towards assuming that New Testament Christians viewed Jesus' miracles in the same way. Thus miracles occupy such a prominent place in the gospels primarily to demonstrate that Jesus is God.

Surprisingly, however, the gospels do not regard the ability to perform miracles in itself as proof of divinity. Recall, for example, the story in which one of the disciples reports to Jesus, "We saw a man driving out demons in your name and we told him to stop, because he was not one of us." Jesus responds, "Do not stop him. No one who does a miracle in my name can in the next moment say anything bad about me, for whoever is not

> ### God Is Not Trapped
>
> "Miracles are evidence that there are dimensions to God that with all our knowledge we have not been able to anticipate. To believe in a miracle is only a way of saying that God is free—free to do a new thing. He is not bound to a deterministic creation of natural cause and effect. He is not trapped in his own cosmic machine. He is free above and beyond what we observe of his ways. . . . The gospel message says: 'You don't live in a mechanistic world ruled by necessity; you don't live in a random world ruled by chance; you live in a world ruled by the God of Exodus and Easter.'"
>
> —Eugene H. Peterson, *Five Smooth Stones for Pastoral Work,* Atlanta: John Knox Press, 1980, p. 139ff.

against us is for us" (Mark 9:38-40). Or recall Jesus' commission to his disciples "to drive out evil spirits and to heal every disease and sickness" (Matt. 10:1). The reason why miracle stories were included in the gospels was not first of all to prove Jesus' divinity but to announce the imminent arrival of the kingdom of God. Miracles are central to Jesus' message that the kingdom of God is near. Miracles anticipate that kingdom. They show what life in the kingdom is like.

But before the kingdom of God can arrive in full, Jesus must first destroy another kingdom—the kingdom of Satan. Jesus' battle with Satan begins in his exorcisms and cures, and climaxes in Jesus' crucifixion and resurrection. Exorcisms are skirmishes—minor fights leading up to a decisive battle. So are the miracles of healing. The very vocabulary the gospels use to describe disease and healing reflects a situation of war. Diseases that may be diagnosed medically as epilepsy (Mark 9:14-29) or as arthritis (Luke 13:10-17) are linked with Satan and his kingdom. In the gospels diseases are treated as personified evil. In Luke 4:39, for example, Jesus rebukes a fever, much as he rebukes demons. Nature miracles too are skirmishes between Jesus and Satan. A good example is the stilling of the storm, when Jesus rebukes the wind (Mark 4:39), just as he rebukes sickness and demons elsewhere. In summary, in the gospels all miracles are invasions of the kingdom of Satan for the purpose of overthrowing it and establishing the kingdom of God in its place.

Quick Orientation

To develop an awareness of the pervasive presence of miracles in the gospels and to show that miracle stories are an integral part of the gospels, we will take a quick look at the opening chapters of Mark—the oldest of the four gospels. Before recording his first series of miracles, Mark reports the baptism and the temptation of Jesus (1:9-13). At the baptism the Spirit of God comes upon Jesus. At once Jesus enters the desert to face temptations; the temptation is Jesus' first skirmish with Satan. Then, empowered by the Spirit, Jesus goes forth to proclaim the good news: "The kingdom of God is near." God's kingly rule is about to break in and wrest away Satan's power. It is not surprising, therefore, that Mark's first miracle is an exorcism. Next, in Mark 1:31, Jesus heals Simon's mother-in-law of a fever. In 1:32-34 Jesus cures *many* who are sick and casts out *many* demons. In 1:39 he casts out more demons. In 1:40 he heals a leper and in 2:11 a paralytic. In 3:10-11 more sick people are healed and more demons are exorcised. Then, in 3:22-30, Mark spells out clearly the meaning of the exorcisms: They are struggles between the Spirit of God and the power of Satan. Exorcisms make Satan impotent. In 4:35-41 Jesus rebukes the wind, and 5:1-20 tells the story of a man occupied by so many demons that his name is Legion. On and on Mark goes. In fact, out of a total of 666 verses, some 209 verses deal with miracles. Mark's gospel is saturated with miraculous action, moving from exorcisms to healings to nature miracles. Ralph P. Martin thinks Mark's pace has a special attraction: "A generation which gets action-packed drama on the TV news with on-the-spot coverage and instant news analysis is bound to be drawn to this Gospel—if it is drawn to any of the Church's holy books" (*Where the Action Is*, Glendale, Calif.: Regal Books, 1977, p. 6).

An Exorcism

According to one tally that does not count parallels or variants of a miracle story present in another gospel, the four gospels contain a total of six exorcisms, seventeen healings (often more than one person), and eight nature miracles. In the remainder of this chapter we will study one or more representative examples of each. First of all, let us examine the story of the demoniac recorded in Mark 5:1-20, Matthew 8:28-34, and Luke 8:26-39.

A Folk Story?

This incident is often regarded as a grotesque and farcical folk story that reflects first-century superstition and demonology and that therefore need not be taken too seriously. Jesus outsmarts the demons by acceding to their request to transfer to a herd of pigs. But even the unclean pigs cannot endure their presence and so rush to destroy themselves in the sea. Many people react to this story by saying: Sorry, but under the impact of modern psychology and psychiatry we no longer believe in personal demons. What this story calls demon possession we now call neurosis or psychosis. This modern way of explaining the story makes Jesus a good psychologist, which undoubtedly he was. Still, it misses the point of the story. Whenever Jesus speaks of demons he is not using a figure of speech. Jesus does not just speak *about* demons; he speaks to demons and engages them in combat. When Jesus casts out demons, two kingdoms engage in combat. On the outcome of this combat hinges the success of Jesus' ministry. "If I drive out demons by the Spirit of God," Jesus says in Matthew 12:28, "then the kingdom of God has come upon you."

Comparing Mark and Matthew

Biblical scholars generally agree that both Matthew and Luke got their stories from Mark—the earliest of the three gospels. Luke reproduces Mark's story without any substantial changes and without introducing a new perspective. This, however, is not true of Matthew. Matthew reduces Mark's twenty verses to a mere seven, omitting the account of the demoniac's conduct (Mark 5:3-5), the dialogue between Jesus and the demon (Mark 5:9), the encounter between the people of the city and the healed demoniac (Mark 5:15-16), and the conversation between Jesus and the healed man who wants to follow Jesus (Mark 5:18-20). The total effect of these omissions is to highlight Jesus' victory over the demons. Matthew takes no interest in the healing of the demoniac; he concentrates exclusively on the destruction of the demons. Though in Mark the demon pleads, "Swear to God that you won't torture me!" in Matthew the demons accuse Jesus of having come to torture them "before the appointed time," that is, before the full coming of the kingdom of God. In Matthew the demons are saying in effect that with Jesus the kingdom of God has already come. They clearly understand the purpose of Jesus' mission—something that cannot be said of the people of the city who are completely blind to Jesus' victory over the demons, seeing him only as a destroyer of their local economy. So Matthew ends the story with the people begging Jesus to go away. Mark, on the other hand, ends his story with Jesus telling the healed man to go home and tell his family how much the Lord has done for him. Still, for both Matthew and Mark, the essential point of the encounter is Jesus' victory over the demons.

Cast Out Demons!

"[T]he words of our text ['Cast out the demons'] remain valid. They belong to the message of the Christ, and they tell us about something that belongs to the Christ as the Christ—the power to conquer the demonic forces that control our lives, mind and body. And I believe that, of all the different ways to communicate the message of the Christ to others, this way will prove to be the most adequate for the people of our time. It is something they can understand. For in every country of the world, including our own, there is an awareness of the power of evil as has not existed for centuries."

—Paul Tillich, *The Eternal Now,* New York: Charles Scribner's Sons, 1962, p. 60.

Two Healings

Jesus explains his healings in response to John the Baptist's question, "Are you the one who is to come or should we expect someone else?" Jesus' answer is "Go back and report to John what you hear and see: The blind receive sight, the lame walk, those who have leprosy are cured, the deaf hear" (Matt. 11:3-4). Jesus refers John to Isaiah 35 where the dawning of the age of salvation is said to be visible in the healing of the blind, the deaf, the lame, and the dumb. In applying Isaiah 35 to his work of healing, Jesus claims that his miracles signal the dawn of the age of salvation. Things are moving. The kingdom of God is near.

The Healing of the Paralytic
(Mark 2:1-12; Matt. 9:1-8; Luke 5:17-26)

Most of us know the story of the paralytic as it is found in Mark. Four men lower a paralytic through an opening in the roof above Jesus. When Jesus sees their faith, he says to the paralytic, "Son, your sins are forgiven." Hearing this, some teachers of the law think, "He's blaspheming. Who can forgive sins but God alone?" Then, to show that he has authority to forgive sins, Jesus says to the paralytic, "Get up!" Luke's version is close to Mark's, but Matthew's is not. Matthew is more concerned with the forgiveness of sins than with the miracle itself. So he omits nonessential people and actions. This is Matthew's way of interpreting what goes on. To Matthew, the dialogue exchange of ideas about forgiveness matters most. Thus, the organizing center of his account is Jesus' authority to forgive sins. Also, the crowd's praising of God does not refer, as it does in Mark, to the miracle as such but rather to the fact that God has given to human beings the authority to forgive sins.

In all three gospel accounts, Jesus tells the paralytic that his sins are forgiven—before Jesus heals him. Sin, not sickness, is the paralytic's real problem. Jesus has authority to deal with both. He has authority both to forgive and to heal. The roots of this authority go back to Jesus' mission to preach the coming of the kingdom of God. The forgiveness of sins is at the center of this preaching. Unless people are forgiven, how can they enter the kingdom? But although Jesus' act of healing the paralytic does not elicit charges of blasphemy, his words of forgiveness do—even though both healing and forgiveness flow from his single authority. Jesus' power to heal and his power to forgive are but two dimensions of his single mission to make people fit for the kingdom. The teachers of the law, however, see the former as legitimate and the latter as illegitimate. They object not to the healing but to the forgiveness of sins: "Who can forgive sins but God alone?"

The Sickness of Sin

"The Gospels depict Jesus as having spent a surprising amount of time healing people. Although, like the author of Job before him, he specifically rejected the theory that sickness was God's way of getting even with sinners (John 9:1-3), he nonetheless seems to have suggested a connection between sickness and sin, almost to have seen sin as a kind of sickness. 'Those who are well have no need of a physician, but those who are sick,' he said. 'I came not to call the righteous but sinners' (Mark 2:17). This is entirely compatible, of course, with the Hebrew view of man as a psychosomatic unity, an indivisible amalgam of body and soul whereby if either goes wrong, the other is affected."

—Frederick Buechner, *Wishful Thinking*, New York: Harper & Row, 1973, p. 35ff.

Was Jesus' act of forgiveness God's work or not? After all, no one can *see* the forgiveness of sins. What you *can* see, however, is the healing of someone who is paralyzed. So, this healing makes visible the coming of the kingdom of God. Thus when Jesus heals the paralytic, he proves at the same time that his words of forgiveness open the kingdom. What Jesus in effect is saying to the paralytic is, "But look, my poor man, now you have met *me* and I have the authority to take your hand and put it back into the hand of the Father. By my word I can open the closed door of the Father's house for you; look, it's opening now. I say to you, it's opening, and you are God's child again" (Helmut Thielicke, *Man in God's World*, New York: Harper & Row, 1963, p. 121ff).

The Healing of Blind Bartimaeus
(Mark 10:46-52; Matt. 20:29-34; Luke 18:35-43)

The story of Bartimaeus appears in three somewhat different versions. Mark's version is generally considered the original one; Matthew's and Luke's are considered later editions. Luke somewhat modifies Mark's account while Matthew, characteristically, omits from his account all secondary people and nonessential descriptive details. But neither Matthew nor Luke introduces anything really new, so our discussion will center on Mark's setting of the story of Bartimaeus.

To understand the story in greater depth, we must see it against the background of Old Testament prophecy. According to the writings of the prophets, the opening of blind eyes is one of the signs heralding the arrival of the day of the Lord. "In that day . . . the eyes of the blind will see" (Isa. 29:18; see also 35:5). Thus, Jesus' opening of blind eyes is his way of saying: The day of the Lord is at hand! The kingdom of God is near!

To understand the Bartimaeus story we must also be aware of its pivotal place in the gospel of Mark as a whole. The healing of Bartimaeus concludes the central section of the gospel, Mark 8:22-10:52. In this central section no one recognizes Jesus. All are totally blind to who Jesus really is. This is why Mark both begins and ends this section with the healing of a blind person, the only two such healings in Mark. Mark 8:22-26 reports the healing of a man who is blind in Bethsaida and 10:45-52 that of Bartimaeus. Within the brackets of these two healings, Peter, representing all the disciples, has his blindness partly cured near Caesarea Philippi. Here he sees that Jesus is the Messiah (8:29), even though he still fails to see that Jesus must suffer and die and rise again. Following that, Jesus three times predicts his forthcoming passion and resurrection (8:31; 9:31; 10:32), and God announces to Peter, James, and John from the cloud, "This is my Son, whom I love" (9:7). But still the disciples remain blind to what Jesus must accomplish in Jerusalem. So by placing the story of Bartimaeus at the conclusion of the central section, Mark loads it with additional meaning. Bartimaeus, in a real sense, personifies the disciples. Though he calls Jesus "Son of David," or Israel's political Messiah, Bartimaeus is blind to what lies ahead in Jerusalem. And just as the healed Bartimaeus follows Jesus to Jerusalem, so also the disciples follow Jesus to Jerusalem. In addition, the healing of Bartimaeus right before the passion prefigures the full healing of the disciples' sight that will enable them to see Jesus as the Messiah who must suffer and die and rise again.

The restoration of Bartimaeus' sight points to Jesus' passion in still another way: "It is only when the centurion *sees* the dead Jesus on the cross—just as the temple veil is rent—that he sees the ultimate truth: the crucified Jesus is revealed as the Son of God: 'This man truly was God's son' (15:39). For the first time in the Gospel, a human being can say in faith that Jesus is the Son of God; only the 'theophany' of the cross makes this vision of faith possible" (*A Marginal Jew,* vol. 2, p. 687).

Two Nature Miracles

Jesus Changes Water into Wine (John 2:1-11)

In the gospel of John are seven miracles:

- changing water into wine (2:1-11)
- healing an official's son (4:46-54)
- healing an invalid at the Bethesda pool (5:1-18)
- feeding the five thousand (6:1-15)
- walking on the water (6:16-21)
- healing a blind man (9:1-41)
- raising Lazarus (11:1-57)

Although in the gospel of John Jesus himself refers to his miracles as "works," all others refer to them as signs. Of course, the Old Testament is the main reference for understanding signs. Here God, for example, performs miraculous signs through Moses (Ex. 10:1). Moses' staff turning into a snake is a sign, because it points beyond itself to the power of Moses' God. Similarly in the gospel of John, each of Jesus' miracles is a sign. Each sign stands for who Jesus is. Each sign reveals his glory. Each sign points forward to his death and resurrection where his full glory is revealed. No one who rejects Jesus' signs comes to faith in him. Signs are the open door through which people come to Jesus. And signs fulfill their purpose only when they lead people to believe that "Jesus is the Christ, the Son of God" (John 20:31).

The first sign Jesus performs is turning water into wine. Like Jesus' inaugural sermon in the Nazareth synagogue (Luke 4:14-21), this sign reveals the purpose of Jesus' ministry. In the sign at Cana, Jesus discloses what his mission is. His mission is changing water into wine; it is changing the religion of the Law, symbolized by water, into the religion of the gospel, symbolized by wine.

And notice that the very next story, the account of the cleansing of the Temple (John 2:12-22), is a commentary on the Cana story. Jesus has come to replace the center of the religion of the Law, the Jerusalem temple. When the Jews demand a sign to prove his authority to cleanse the temple, Jesus replies, "Destroy this temple, and I will raise it again in three days" (2:19). In other words, Jesus' risen body replaces the Jerusalem temple. The risen Jesus is the "place" where God and people meet in spirit and in truth. The fact that John places the temple story at the beginning of his gospel, immediately following the Cana story, is significant.

The first three gospels include the temple incident as part of the passion story. In Mark and Matthew the story of the temple cleansing has the purpose of explaining why Jesus had to die. The false witnesses at Jesus' trial reported that Jesus threatened to destroy the temple and rebuild it in three days (Mark 14:58; Matt. 26:61). And this report is one of the reasons why Jesus is condemned to die.

But things are different in John. Here Jesus' death is from above, not from below. Here no one takes Jesus' life from him; he lays it down of his own accord (John 10:18), dying when "his hour" has come. So John places the temple story at the beginning of his gospel, not for chronological but for theological reasons. In John the story of the temple cleansing is a powerful illustration of Jesus' mission to change the water of the law into the wine of the gospel.

John describes the miracle at Cana as "the first of his miraculous signs" through which Jesus reveals his glory (2:11). This first sign introduces a whole series of signs that progressively reveal Jesus' glory—the glory he had with the Father "before the world began" (17:5). This glory begins to shine forth from Jesus at the time of his incarnation (1:14). It is first revealed to the disciples at Cana. It shines forth most brightly in his death on the cross at the divinely appointed "hour" (2:4). For when Jesus says to his mother, "My hour has not yet come," he is referring to the hour when he will be lifted up on the cross. Changing water into wine is a preliminary sign pointing to this culminating manifestation of Jesus' glory.

Jesus Stills the Storm (Mark 4:35-41; Matt. 8:23-27)

Our second example of a nature miracle is Jesus' stilling of the storm. A comparison of this story in Mark and Matthew reveals significant differences. In Mark, the story is a nature miracle. It marks the end of a chapter almost entirely taken up by parables and the beginning of a series of miracle stories. In Matthew the context is different. Matthew takes the story he finds in Mark and retells it in such a way that the focus is not on the miracle, the way it is in Mark, but on discipleship. The ship becomes a symbol for the community of disciples—the church. The church for which Matthew writes his gospel is a church that is going through stormy times and whose life is marked by change and confusion. Therefore, before he tells about the storm, Matthew first tells the story of two would-be disciples (8:19-22): a teacher of the law and another man, one of Jesus' disciples. Surprisingly, Jesus does not react to their offer with enthusiasm. Instead, he discourages both men by pointing out what following him means. Being Jesus' disciple means not having a place to call home. It means resetting priorities. Following Jesus comes before family obligations. Whoever wants to follow Jesus must know before-hand what's required.

It is at this point that Matthew's story of the storm begins. The miracle at sea is no longer of first importance, as it is in Mark. What is important is what awaits those who follow Jesus into the storm. In Mark the disciples take Jesus along in the boat; in Matthew Jesus "got into the boat and his disciples followed him" (8:23). Then, without warning, a furious storm comes up on the sea. But Jesus is sleeping. The disciples wake him and say, "Lord, save us! We're going to drown!" In Mark the cry for help is just that; in Matthew it is a prayer. In Mark the disciples call Jesus "Teacher"; in Matthew, "Lord."

Discipleship, Matthew is saying, is confessing Jesus' lordship in the midst of a storm. Now the Greek language has two words for storm: *lailaps* and *seismos*. *Lailaps* is the usual word, the word used in weather reports. Mark calls the storm a *lailaps*. *Seismos* is the unusual word. The New Testament uses it to designate apocalyptic events. Jesus, for example, warns that at the end of the age "there will be earthquakes [*seismoi*] in various places" (Mark 13:8). Also in the book of Revelation we read that at the opening of the sixth seal "there was a great earthquake [*seismos*]" (6:12). Here, in the story of the storm, Matthew uses the word *seismos* as a code-word for the terrors at the end of the world, the same way Jesus does when he says that "there will be *seismoi* in various places." The word *seismos* carries the idea that demonic powers are being unleashed and tribulations are sweeping over our lives. By choosing this word over *lailaps* Matthew is telling us this: what the disciples are experiencing in their fishing boat on the lake is symbolic of the end-time tribulation that those who follow Jesus will experience. But, Matthew assures us at the same time, the boat into which we follow Jesus is unsinkable. The powers of hell cannot prevail against it, for Jesus is on board and he has the power to command the storm to be still.

Jesus on Board

"Jesus Christ is always where we are, where the winds howl and the breakers pour down upon us. He came into the world homeless and had no place where he could lay his head. The homeless and forsaken can know: this man is with me. . . . He who must die can know: this man too tasted the pangs of death and will be my brother as I launch out on the deep. He who has suffered shipwreck, drifting helplessly on the sea or on the symbolic sea of life can know: he sleeps in my boat too, even though it seems abandoned like a nutshell to the play of the elements. He gives me security and enfolds me with his peace, whether by rebuking the elements or by receiving me in a watery grave and escorting me to eternal joy."

—Helmut Thielicke, *How Modern Should Theology Be?* London: Collins, 1967, p. 57ff.

The ending of the story in Mark reads, "They were terrified and asked each other, 'Who is this? Even the wind and the waves obey him'" (Mark 4:41). Again, the disciples are blind to Jesus' identity, as they are throughout the gospel of Mark. Matthew, whose gospel emphasizes the hidden nature of Jesus' identity less than Mark, slightly modifies what he reads in Mark. Instead of asking, "Who is this?" the disciples ask, "What sort of man is this?"

Jesus brings God's rule. Jesus performs miracles to announce the arrival of the kingdom of God. He exorcises demons to show that where God rules the rule of Satan is no more. He heals the sick to signal the dawn of the age of salvation. He walks the waves and stills the storm to show that all of creation obeys him.

SIGNALING JESUS' RESURRECTION

The Gospels in Focus

The purpose of each gospel—from beginning to end—is to portray the risen Jesus as preached by the apostles. Everything in the gospels is written from the conviction that Jesus rose from the dead. Had there not been that conviction, there would have been no gospels. The gospels fuse fact and faith, historical fact and theological interpretation. They offer an interpreted history. This is no cause for alarm, for *all* history writing is a mix of fact and interpretation. All historians record past events from an interpreting standpoint.

Paul's before-and-after view of Jesus' crucifixion is a clear example of how faith interprets facts. Before his conversion, Paul knew that Jesus had been crucified under Pontius Pilate. But for him this fact was reason to believe that Jesus was an impostor and that the Jesus movement deserved to be wiped out. After his conversion, however, this same fact took on radically different meaning. The converted Paul believed that in Jesus' crucifixion God had reconciled the world to himself. In both instances—both before and after his conversion—Paul interpreted the fact of Jesus' crucifixion. Would modern media have benefited Paul in rightly interpreting Jesus' crucifixion? Would they have helped him ferret out what precisely took place on Good

Friday and Easter morning? No, because no whirring TV camera or reporters' professional eye could have focused on what was actually going on. All they would have been able to do is report the external facts. To understand the internal facts requires faith.

No Resurrection, No Gospel

"We are tempted to believe that, although the Resurrection may be the climax of the Gospel, there is yet a Gospel that stands upon its own feet and may be understood and appreciated before we pass on to the Resurrection. The first disciples did not find it so. For them the Gospel without the Resurrection was not merely a Gospel without its final chapter: it was not a Gospel at all. Jesus Christ had, it is true, taught and done great things, but he did not allow the disciples to rest in these things. He led them on to paradox, perplexity and darkness; and there he left them. There too they would have remained, had he not been raised from death. But his Resurrection threw its own light backwards upon the death and the ministry that went before; it illuminated the paradoxes and disclosed the unity of his words and deeds."

—Michael Ramsey, *The Resurrection of Christ*, London: Collins, 1961, p. 9.

A person needs faith to penetrate the inner core of Jesus' crucifixion and resurrection. And this is precisely the medium the gospel writers used. Their faith interprets historical facts. Because the gospel writers believe in Jesus' resurrection, it is not surprising that some gospel miracle stories anticipate and portray the resurrected Jesus. Having been shaped by Easter faith, these stories naturally give hints of what the risen Jesus will be like. Five of these stories are the raising of Jairus' daughter, Jesus' walking on the water, the raising of the young man of Nain, the raising of Lazarus, and Jesus' transfiguration. Although two of these stories can be found in only one of the gospels, all five stories signal Jesus' resurrection. In each story the risen Jesus shines through a portrait of the earthly Jesus.

Jesus Raises Jairus' Daughter
(Mark 5:21-43; Matt. 9:18-26; Luke 8:40-56)

The story of Jairus' daughter is like a Russian doll. When you open it, it contains another doll. When you open the story of Jairus' daughter, it contains the story of the woman with the discharge of blood. Both stories are resurrection stories. Jairus' daughter is raised physically; the woman with the discharge is raised socially. You recall how Jesus' trip to the house of

Jairus is interrupted by a woman "who had been subject to bleeding for twelve years." Her condition makes her and all she touches unclean. According to Leviticus 15:25-26, "When a woman has a discharge of blood for many days at a time other than her monthly period . . . she will be unclean as long as she has the discharge. . . . Any bed she lies on while her discharge continues will be unclean. . . . and anything she sits on will be unclean." She must stay out of everybody's way. The prevalent Jewish idea of holiness makes her a social outcast.

Of course, the people of Israel are to be the holy people of God. To be holy, they must separate themselves from all uncleanness. For uncleanness is not simply a lack of cleanness; it is a defiling power—at least, so everyone in Jesus' day is told.

Jesus, however, redefines holiness; he transforms its meaning. To Jesus, holiness is contagious—not uncleanness. To Jesus, holiness is a transforming power—not a power needing protection. This radically new understanding of holiness "underlies the account of the healing of the woman with a discharge in Mark 5:25-34. Her condition rendered her and all that she touched unclean (Lev. 15:25-30). Yet when she touched Jesus' garment, it was not uncleanness that was transferred, but rather 'power went forth' from Jesus (5:30) and she was healed" (Marcus J. Borg, *Conflict, Holiness and Politics in the Teaching of Jesus,* p. 148).

> ### Who Touched Me?
>
> "Christian living, at its root, I find admirably symbolized in the Gospel story of the bleeding woman. Jesus Christ is here, is really present among us. That living presence makes it possible for me to reach out to him, to touch the hem of his garment. If I do, he turns to me, looks for me, wants me to know him, yearns to live in me. The faith I showed in touching him begins to make me whole. It is the overture of an exchange that should mark my whole life."
>
> —Walter J. Burghardt, *Sir, We Would Like to See Jesus,* New York: Paulist Press, 1982, p. 102.

After the healing of the woman, the story of Jairus' daughter resumes. Messengers arrive with the news of the girl's death. Soon after, Jesus arrives on the scene. Accompanied by the parents and three of his disciples, Jesus enters the room where the child lies, takes her hand, and speaks to her as though to a sleeping child: "Little girl, get up!" With these words Jesus reveals that the kingdom of God is at hand, for where God rules death must flee. Immediately the girl stands up and walks around.

As we've seen earlier, modern biblical scholars have demonstrated rather conclusively that Mark is the first gospel to have been written and that both Matthew and Luke used Mark as one of their written sources, generally following Mark's narrative outline and often quoting him verbatim. Matthew and Luke knew Mark's account of the story of Jairus' daughter and incorporated it into their own gospel.

After raising the little girl, Mark's Jesus orders the disciples and others "not to let anyone know about this" (5:43), just as after the transfiguration he orders his disciples not to tell anyone about this "until the Son of Man had risen from the dead" (9:9). As the transfiguration makes sense only in the light of Jesus' resurrection, Mark is saying, so does the raising of Jairus' daughter. In Luke, Jesus' order is addressed only to the parents of the girl. Jesus tells them "not to tell anyone what had happened" (8:56). Luke's rewording of Jesus' order as found in Mark, however, creates somewhat of a problem. In Mark, Jesus' order makes sense, for it accords with Mark's scheme of keeping the identity of Jesus as the Messiah a secret. But in Luke there is no such secret. Why then should the parents keep the raising of their daughter a secret? Also, how can the parents possibly *not* tell others about it? We are left to wonder why Jesus doesn't tell the parents what he tells the demoniac he healed: "[T]ell how much God has done for you" (Luke 8:39).

Jesus Walks on the Water
(Mark 6:45-52; Matt. 14:22-33; John 6:16-24)

The story of Jesus walking on the water should not be read as a sea-rescue story. The disciples do not find themselves in danger of drowning. Though the wind is against them, there are no waves breaking over the boat that make the disciples cry out in fear of their lives. When they do cry out it is at the sight of Jesus, for they think he is a ghost. Central to the story is "the sea"—an image that suggests a threatening force opposed to God. When the ancient Hebrews wished to stress God's power, they often spoke of God displaying power over the sea. God alone "treads on the waves of the sea" (Job 9:8). God alone rules "over the surging sea" (Ps. 89:9). At the time of the exodus from Egypt, God "made a road in the depths of the sea so that the redeemed might cross over" (Isa. 51:10). Therefore, when we read that Jesus walks on the sea, we are given to understand that he shares in the power of God. What is said of God in the Old Testament is now said of Jesus.

The story of Jesus walking on the sea can be found in Mark, Matthew, and John; Luke omits it. Although Matthew basically follows Mark, there are some important differences.

Mark's language is reminiscent of Old Testament theophany or manifestation of God; Matthew's language shows similarities to that of Jesus' post-resurrection appearances. Reading Mark's story as a theophany helps explain, for example, the otherwise puzzling sentence: "He was about to pass by them" (Mark 6:48). What prompts Jesus to go out to the disciples in the first place is his seeing that they were straining at the oars because the wind was against them. Why then would he pass by them once he got to them? For the answer we must go to the stories of Moses in Exodus 33:12-23 and Elijah in 1 Kings 19:9-18. When Moses asks God to show his glory, God answers, "I will cause all my goodness to pass in front of [by] you, and I will proclaim my name, the Lord, in your presence" (33:19). In Elijah's case, God instructs him to stand on the mountain in his presence, "for the Lord is about to pass by" (19:11). The Old Testament phrase "to pass by someone," writes John P. Meier, "illumines the point that Mark is making in verse 48: Jesus wished to reveal himself to his disciples in all his divine power and majesty by demonstrating his dominion over the unruly forces of wind, sea, and waves. He acts toward them as Yahweh . . . acts in the Old Testament" (*A Marginal Jew,* vol. 2, p. 907).

In contrast to Mark, Matthew tells the story in language similar to that of post-resurrection stories. Thus he drops Mark's sentence, "He was about to pass by them," and adds the story of Peter walking toward Jesus on the water—a story that reminds us of the post-Easter appearance in John 21:1-14. In both Matthew's and John's stories Peter is the first to identify Jesus. In both stories Peter walks toward Jesus, walking upon the water in Matthew's story and wading through the water in John's story. When Peter begins to sink and cries out, "Lord, save me!" Jesus rebukes Peter for doubting. The same tension between faith and doubt is present in Matthew 28:17 when the eleven disciples see the risen Jesus but some doubt. Another example is Matthew's concluding scene of Jesus' climbing into the boat. It too recalls a resurrection appearance. For when we read that Jesus climbs into the boat and the wind dies down and all in the boat worship Jesus, saying, "Truly you are the Son of God" (14:32-33), we recall the post-resurrection scene in Matthew 28:9 when Jesus suddenly meets the women coming from the tomb and the women "worshiped him."

It's a Ghost!

"Matthew recorded this story [of Jesus walking on the water] when the church was in stormy seas. Jesus had not returned in the way that the early Christians expected, and the reign of God appeared to be drowning amid the growing persecution of believers and their internal squabbles. . . . Maybe Christ is not coming to us in the way we expect, just as Christ did not come to Matthew's community in the way they expected. Maybe Christ is walking to us across the deep in the ideas and the people who frighten us, who threaten our ideas of how God will be made known."

—Thomas H. Troeger, *The Parable of Ten Preachers*, Nashville: Abingdon Press, 1992, p. 120ff.

Mark's concluding statement of the story of Jesus walking on the water comes as a surprise. After Jesus climbs into the boat the disciples are completely amazed, "for they had not understood about the loaves; their hearts were hardened" (Mark 6:52). Mark, then, links the story of Jesus walking on the sea to the preceding story of the miraculous feeding (6:30-44). Because the disciples had failed to penetrate the mystery of Jesus' identity after seeing him multiply the loaves, they are not now in a position to recognize him as he manifests his divine power and glory. Not until Jesus' power breaks the bonds of death and his glory shines on Easter morning will they understand who it was who said to them that night: "Take courage! It is I. Don't be afraid."

Jesus Raises a Widow's Son (Luke 7:11-17)

This story occurs only in the gospel of Luke. What's striking about it is its place in Luke's gospel. Luke puts it in 7:11-17 rather than elsewhere because here it anticipates the story that immediately follows—the story of two messengers sent by John the Baptist to ask Jesus, "Are you the one who was to come, or should we expect someone else?" (7:19).

The bewilderment shining through John's question is not hard to understand when we remember the sad history of the Jews. Ever since the reign of the Seleucid king, Antiochus IV Epiphanes (175-163 B.C.), peace had been notoriously absent from the Jewish realm. Antiochus pursued a policy that drove the Jews to outright rebellion. He "zealously fostered all things Hellenic, which included the worship of Zeus and other Greek gods . . . and also of himself as the visible manifestation of Zeus" (John Bright, *A History of Israel*, Philadelphia: Westminster Press, 1959, p. 403). Antiochus's policy culminated in his edict forbidding the practice of Judaism. He ordered all copies of the Torah destroyed and all temple sacrifices suspended. To crown it all, he introduced the cult of Zeus into the Jerusalem temple. Soon Jews rose in arms against him. That they were able to do so successfully and establish a kingdom of their own was due in large measure to the leadership of Mattathias and his son Judas, called "Maccabeus" (meaning "the hammer"). Judas Maccabeus turned Jewish resistance into a full-scale struggle for independence. But the Maccabean kingdom that developed from this struggle eventually collapsed under the weight of internal violence and was followed by the rule of Herod the Great. Fully subservient to Rome, Herod furthered the aim of Caesar Augustus to establish a uniform Greek-Roman civilization in the entire empire. Then, after Herod's death in 4 B.C., Augustus divided the Jewish kingdom among Herod's three sons. One of these, Archelaus, ruled Judea and Samaria for ten years, after which Judea became a Roman province under a Roman procurator. Herod's second son, Herod Antipas, ruled Galilee and Perea from 4 B.C. to A.D. 39.

As far as Jewish eyes could see, Israel was beyond political redemption. Despair ruled. The only remaining hope was for a completely new kingdom ruled by the Messiah. But in the days of John the Baptist even this hope was all mixed up. The older prophets spoke of a glorious time when God himself would come down, destroy Israel's enemies, and establish justice and peace; at this time a wise and powerful king of David's house would reign on behalf of God. Newer prophets spoke of the Messiah's rule as worldwide. Other prophets called for moral purification. Still others held that the Messiah would rule only over a remnant of Israel. All this is part of John's bewildered cry: Tell me, will the present desperate situation continue? Are you the one whom Israel expects? If you are, then why not do your job? Why not take your throne and rescue us?

It is in answer to this question that Jesus says, "Go back and report to John what you have seen and heard: The blind receive sight, the lame walk, those who have leprosy are cured, the deaf hear, the dead are raised" (Luke 7:22). But it is here that Luke faces a problem. Thus far Luke has reported that Jesus healed various kinds of sickness (4:40), drove out demons (4:35, 41), healed a leper (5:13), and made a paralytic walk (5:24), but he has not yet reported that Jesus raised a dead person. This most likely is the reason why Luke inserts the story of Jesus raising the young man of Nain right before he answers the question of John the Baptist. The story anticipates Jesus' claim that he raises the dead (7:22). It anticipates one more thing. It also anticipates God raising Jesus from the dead. For, as Fred B. Craddock writes, "all Christians reading Luke 7:11-17 have their minds run ahead to the climax of the Gospel: God raises Jesus from the dead. Luke must have had similar thoughts; after all, the whole story of Jesus is being narrated from the perspective of one who is looking back through an empty tomb" (*Luke,* Louisville: John Knox Press, 1990, p. 98).

Jesus Raises Lazarus (John 11:1-44)

The story of Jesus and Lazarus—one of the most moving stories in the gospels—is found only in the gospel of John. It portrays a Jesus who is significantly different from the Jesus of the other gospels. In the other gospels, Jesus' miracles point beyond himself to the kingdom of God. The emphasis throughout is on the power of God that overcomes the power of Satan. But John does not present the ministry of Jesus in those terms. In fact, he talks very little about the kingdom and Satan. Though John is quite aware of the opposition of Satan (13:27; 14:30), he does not emphasize the connection between the miracles and the destruction of Satan's power. In John's gospel, Jesus' miracles point to his divine identity. Miracles are intended to evoke faith in Jesus as the giver of undying life. As John himself says, the reason he records seven of Jesus' miraculous signs is "that you may believe that Jesus is the Christ, the Son of God, and that by believing you may have life in his name" (20:31).

The story of Jesus and Lazarus concludes the first half of John's gospel—the half devoted to the seven signs performed by Jesus. Jesus is not a wonder worker; he performs signs. Wonders point to themselves; signs point away from themselves. John's gospel sketches the ministry of Jesus as a series of signs, and the raising of Lazarus is the last and greatest of these signs. John has carefully arranged the seven signs to create a crescendo. Each of the earlier signs conveys "to some degree the message clearly proclaimed by this final sign: Jesus is the giver of life. The life he gives is not ordinary human life; it is . . . God's own life, eternal life, communicated right now to believers who accept Jesus as the savior signified by the signs he performs" (John

P. Meier, *A Marginal Jew*, vol. 2, p. 798). The miracle of raising Lazarus is not an end in itself. It is not just performed for the sake of Lazarus and his sisters. No, says Jesus, "it is for God's glory so that God's Son may be glorified through it" (John 11:4).

Raising Lazarus is a sign pointing forward to the resurrection of Jesus himself. This is symbolically portrayed in the different ways in which Lazarus and Jesus emerge from the tomb. Jesus rises never to die again. Therefore he leaves behind in the tomb the strips of linen and the burial cloth that have been around his head (20:6-7). Lazarus rises to die again. He therefore emerges from the tomb with "his hands and feet wrapped with strips of linen, and a cloth around his face" (11:44).

As a sign, the raising of Lazarus points not merely to the future resurrection age but also to Jesus as the one in whom this future age is already present. When Jesus says to Martha, "Your brother will rise again" (11:23), Martha, drawing on her childhood training, says, "I know he will rise again in the resurrection at the last day." Jesus then tells her: What you hope for at the last day is already present now. In me the promised future has already arrived. In fact, I am that future. Do you believe this, Martha? Do you believe that by believing in me you have already experienced resurrection, because I myself, here and now, am the resurrection and the life that does not die?

Frederick D. Maurice, a nineteenth-century British theologian, once said that this exchange between Jesus and Martha depressed him. How sad, Maurice said, that after some 1,800 years the church has gotten most Christians to the point to which the synagogue got Martha: resurrection in the future. Only a handful have ever gotten past that point and made the leap of faith that Jesus got Martha to make—the leap to resurrection here and now. And yet that leap is all over the pages of the New Testament.

> ## God of Dead Ends
>
> The story of Jesus and Lazarus brings to mind the story of Sonia the prostitute and Raskolnikov the murderer in Dostoevski's novel *Crime and Punishment*. A most moving scene in that novel is when Sonia reads the story of Lazarus to Raskolnikov. Sonia knows the story by heart, for this is *her* story. She explains to Raskolnikov what it means to be a prostitute. It is living death. But she also explains what it means to know that Jesus can raise from death. I cannot raise myself from death, she says. I cannot lift myself out of the profession into which I have sunk under the pressure of family poverty. My only hope is the miracle of resurrection. "What would I be," Sonia asks, "without the God who raised up Lazarus, who in a wondrous miracle can also raise me from death to life?"

Jesus Is Transfigured
(Mark 9:2-8; Matt. 17:1-8; Luke 9:28-36)

To make sense out of the story of Jesus' transfiguration, we must begin by reading Mark 8:31 or its almost identical parallel passages in Matthew 16:21 and Luke 9:22. These passages provide us with the proper perspective from which to view the happenings on the high mountain. They record the first prediction of Jesus' passion and speak of the "must" of Jesus' suffering, rejection, death, and resurrection. Note that both Matthew and Luke join Mark in placing the story of the transfiguration right after this first prediction of the passion. The transfiguration has strategic importance; it closes Jesus' Galilean ministry and prepares for his journey to Jerusalem where certain death awaits.

On top of a high mountain Jesus is "metamorphosed" (this is the actual word used in the Greek!). Jesus' *morphe,* or form, is changed so that it starts to shine. So do his garments. Time also changes. It loses its limits and sequence. Moses and Elijah, who lived in different centuries, appear. Why do *these* two figures appear from Israel's past? Most likely because in Jewish tradition these two men were believed not to have died but to have ascended directly to heaven without the pain of suffering and death. According to the Old Testament, "Elijah went up to heaven in a whirlwind" (2 Kings 2:11). And of Moses it says that after he died the Lord himself buried him and that the place of his burial is unknown (Deut. 34:5-6). From the account in Deuteronomy 34, Jewish theologians concluded that Moses had been given a special exit from life, similar to Elijah's. These theologians reasoned that if God had *buried* Moses, God must have previously taken him to heaven. Both Elijah and Moses, then, had been able to accomplish their mission without having to suffer and die. Peter's words, "Let us put up three shelters—one for you, one for

> **August 6**
>
> "In the Eastern church calendar, August 6 is the Feast of the Transfiguration. . . . In the Western secular calendar, August 6 is the anniversary of the dropping of the first atomic bomb on Hiroshima. Each anniversary exemplifies a certain kind of power that brought about a certain kind of 'transfiguration' that changed the course of history."
>
> —Robert M. Brown, *Unexpected News,* Philadelphia: Westminster Press, 1984, p. 125ff.

Moses and one for Elijah" (Mark 9:5), show that Peter classifies Jesus with Moses and Elijah. He thinks of them as three of a kind. In spite of what Jesus has taught him (see Mark 8:31), Peter persists in his mistaken notion that Jesus, like Elijah and Moses before him, will be able to accomplish his mission without having to suffer and die. What takes place on the mountain of transfiguration refutes Peter's mistaken notion. Before Jesus can manifest his glory he must first suffer and die. Before there can be Easter there must first be Good Friday.

Both Matthew and Luke add some personal touches to what they read in Mark. Matthew's account, more than Mark's, suggests what will happen when Jesus rises from death. After Jesus is transfigured, for example, we read that "his face shone like the sun" (Matt. 17:2). Revelation 1:16 describes the risen Jesus similarly: "His face was like the sun shining in all its brilliance." Luke's is the only gospel to report on the conversation between Jesus, Moses, and Elijah (9:31-33). In Luke the three speak together of Jesus' approaching suffering and death in Jerusalem. The three disciples, being very sleepy, are not privy to this conversation. But when they are fully awake, they see Jesus' *glory*. Mark and Matthew don't mention Jesus' glory, but Luke does. Previously in Luke, when Peter had confessed Jesus to be "The Christ [or Messiah] of God" (9:20), Jesus had corrected Peter by announcing that he must suffer, be rejected and be killed, and on the third day be raised to life (9:22). Now, on the mountain of transfiguration, Luke confirms both the suffering and the resurrection. Jesus talks about his departure but also appears in glory. Jesus talks about Good Friday but also about Easter.

Throughout the gospels, Jesus' resurrection tends to be anticipated. Some of the gospel stories offer glimpses of the risen and exalted Jesus. They offer hints of what the future will be like.

May

SESSION 8

CALLING FOLLOWERS

Three Circles of Followers

In the gospels of Mark and Matthew, after his baptism by John and temptation by Satan, Jesus calls his first disciples: Simon, Andrew, James, and John. Luke's account is remarkably different. Here Jesus gets into a fishing boat belonging to Simon and teaches from the boat. After he is finished he tells Simon, "Put out into deep water, and let down the nets for a catch" (Luke 5:4). Simon protests that they have been fishing all night without catching anything. Still, he lets down the nets and catches such a large number of fish that the nets begin to break. Seeing this, Peter falls at Jesus' feet and says, "Go away from me, Lord; I am a sinful man" (5:8). Jesus says to Simon, "Don't be afraid; from now on you will catch men" (5:10). Then Simon, James, and John (Luke does not mention Andrew) leave everything and follow Jesus. In Mark and Matthew, the disciples simply follow after being called. In Luke, Jesus first wins their trust by telling them where to catch fish. But in all three gospels the first disciples leave everything and follow Jesus. Not all disciples do, however, for there is more than one circle of disciples.

85

The First Circle

The first circle is the Twelve—those whom Jesus calls to follow him in the strict sense. (Mark, Matthew, and Luke give full lists of the Twelve; the gospel of John refers to the Twelve and names a few but gives no list). Jesus chooses *twelve* disciples to indicate that his mission is to all Israel and that he expects Israel to be fully restored in the coming kingdom. The number twelve symbolizes his mission and his hope.

The Second Circle

Jesus also has a group of followers that is more loosely related to him. In addition to sending out the Twelve (Luke 9:1-11), Jesus sends out the Seventy-Two (Luke 10:1-16) who report great success at getting demons to submit in Jesus' name. This second circle of followers includes many women. Mark, for example, writes that in Galilee, "Mary Magdalene, Mary the mother of James the younger and of Joses, and Salome . . . followed Jesus and cared for his needs" (Mark 15:40-41). Matthew writes that watching the crucifixion from a distance were many women who "had followed Jesus from Galilee to care for his needs" (Matt. 27:55). And Luke writes that many women accompanied Jesus and the Twelve, traveling about from one town and village to another and "helping to support them out of their own means" (Luke 8:3).

The Third Circle

Finally, there is a third circle of followers consisting of people who, for lack of a better word, might be called "sympathizers." They don't follow Jesus on the road, but they follow him at home. Some of these are not identified by name, like the woman who poured very expensive perfume on Jesus' head, but others are Simon the Pharisee (Luke 7:36-50), Zacchaeus (Luke 19:1-10), Joseph of Arimathea who donated a tomb and buried Jesus' body (Mark 15:42-47), and Mary and Martha of Bethany (John 12:1-8).

Though the specific form of following Jesus differs from circle to circle, the substance is the same. It is to lose one's life for Jesus and for the gospel (Mark 8:35). It is to seek first the kingdom Jesus inaugurates (Matt. 6:33). It is to place Jesus above father and mother, spouse and children, brothers and sisters (Luke 9:57-62; 14:26). It is to come to the Father through Jesus who is the way and the truth and the life (John 14:6). Following Jesus is a major theme in all four gospels. Yet, with each gospel addressing the needs of a different community, this theme is formulated differently.

Following Mark's Jesus

Running through the entire gospel of Mark is a sharp contrast between two ways of life: living for oneself and living for others; saving one's life out of fear and losing one's life out of faith. Mark explicitly states these two opposing lifestyles in the center of his gospel, when Jesus is about to begin his final journey to Jerusalem (8:27-10:52). At this point Jesus directly teaches his disciples how God wants them to live. But the disciples resist his teaching. As a result, throughout the journey to Jerusalem Jesus and the disciples clash. Three times on the journey Jesus predicts "that the Son of Man must suffer many things and be rejected by the elders, chief priests and teachers of the law, and that he must be killed and after three days rise again" (8:31; 9:31; 10:33-34). Three times the disciples show that they do not understand or accept Jesus' words. After the first prediction Peter takes Jesus aside and rebukes him (8:32). Jesus' response is, "whoever wants to save his life will lose it, but whoever loses his life for me and for the gospel will save it" (8:35). After the second prediction the disciples, not understanding what Jesus means, are afraid to ask him about it (9:32). But Jesus clarifies his words, saying, "If anyone wants to be first, he must be the very last, and the servant of all" (9:35). After the third prediction James and John request to sit at Jesus' right and left in his glory—showing that they completely miss the point of Jesus' words (10:35-40). Jesus tells them, "whoever wants to become great among you must be your servant, and whoever wants to be first must be slave of all" (10:43-44).

> **Warning and Invitation**
>
> "So the Gospel is a warning as well as an invitation. If you stumble on God and are swept up by desire for his rule, then you must be prepared to shed your cloak, perhaps whole layers of clothing, prepared to be naked as Jesus at Golgotha or the young man in the garden. And the cloaks are not only those of wealth and status, that the rich man and the sons of Zebedee cling to. There are others, of knowledge and experience and religion. As soon as these good things are turned into possessions . . . they impede our road ahead and distract us into the complicated business of defending our property."
>
> —Christopher Burdon, *Stumbling on God*, London: SPCK, 1990, p. 91.

Each of Jesus' responses expresses the contrast between following the world and following Jesus. The way of following the world is acquiring status and power. It is driven by fear. The way of following Jesus is relinquishing power and life. It is energized by faith. The two contrasting lifestyles are saving one's life out of fear and losing one's life out of faith. In the October 1993 issue of *Interpretation*, David Rhoades identifies the following characteristics of these lifestyles:

What People Want for Themselves	What God Wants for People
self-centered	other-centered
save one's own life	lose one's life for the good news
acquire the world	give up possessions
be great	be least
lord over others	be servant to all
be anxious	have faith
fear	courage
harming others	saving others
loyalty to self	loyalty to God for the world

Jesus lives the "what God wants for people" lifestyle. The authorities pursue the "what people want for themselves" lifestyle. The disciples vacillate between these two lifestyles.

Following the World

People who follow the world's standards seek to save their lives (Mark 8:35), to gain the world (8:36), to be first (9:35), and to occupy positions of honor (10:35-40). This quest for power and status is motivated by fear. The Jewish authorities are looking for a way to kill Jesus because they fear him. They fear his popularity and they fear losing their authority over the crowds (11:18; 12:12). The disciples fear too. Even though they have left all and followed Jesus, they often exhibit the same values as non-followers. They follow Jesus in hope of acquiring status and power. They argue about who is greatest among them (9:33-34). And their behavior is marked by fear. They are afraid in the storm (4:40). They are afraid when Jesus is arrested, and desert him and flee (14:50).

Following Jesus

People who live by God's standards are willing to lose their life for Jesus and for the gospel (Mark 8:35), to be the very last and the servant of all (9:35), and to be slave of all (10:44). In the kingdom of God, servants and slaves are models of greatness. The people who embody the values of the kingdom are the poor widow who "out of her poverty put in everything—all she had to live on" (12:44) and the unnamed woman who poured very expensive perfume on Jesus' head (14:3). The disciples sometimes embody these values, for example, when they go out on a mission with "nothing for the journey except a staff—no bread, no bag, no money" (6:8).

Mark's Jesus describes the consequences of following him. Anyone who proclaims the kingly rule of God, he says, is likely to suffer loss and persecution, for this message rouses the powers that are hostile to God's rule. Still, the ultimate consequence of following Jesus is not persecution but resurrection and eternal life in the age to come (10:30).

Mark, it is generally accepted, is addressing his gospel to Christians facing persecution. His basic message to them is, Remember that the Jesus whom you worship as the risen Lord came to that lordship along the road of misunderstanding, humiliation, suffering, and death. And disciples are not above their master. As Jesus' disciples, you must walk the same road. If they persecuted Jesus, they will also persecute you. But just as God vindicated Jesus after suffering, so God will vindicate you. For whoever would save his life will lose it; and whoever loses his life for Jesus' sake and the gospel's will save it.

> ### Getting into Trouble
>
> "We sometimes hear a parent say: 'I want my child brought up in a Christian atmosphere, so that he will stay out of trouble.' There is a grain of truth in that idea. Christian character does overcome or bypass some troubles in life. But can you imagine a parent bringing a child to Jesus with the words: 'I want my boy to go with you, because you will keep him out of trouble'? How might Jesus reply? Perhaps he would say: 'What are you talking about? Foxes have their holes, but I have no place to lay my head. This is no way to avoid trouble' (see Luke 9:57-58). Or he might say: 'Trouble is one thing I can guarantee. If your boy comes with me, he'd better prepare for self-denial, persecution—yes, cruel death.'"
>
> —Roger L. Shinn, *The Sermon on the Mount*, Nashville: Abingdon Press, 1962, p. 23.

Following Matthew's Jesus

Matthew's Jesus calls followers against the backdrop of the Law as laid down in the first five books of the Old Testament. In Matthew, Jesus defines the purpose of his mission as fulfilling the Law (5:17). He commands his disciples to obey the Law's "smallest letter," warns that those who break one of the least of the Law's commandments "will be called least in the kingdom of heaven," and promises that those who practice and teach these commandments "will be called great in the kingdom of heaven" (5:18-19). What matters to Matthew's Jesus is doing God's will as contained in the Law.

But what does this mean? What does Jesus mean when he says that he has come to fulfill the Law?

The Higher Righteousness

The Law Jesus is speaking of is the same Law he quotes to the rich young man who wants to know how to get eternal life. If you want to enter eternal life, Jesus says, obey the commandments: Do not murder, do not commit adultery, do not steal, do not give false testimony, honor your father and mother, and love your neighbor as yourself (19:18-19). All these commandments of the Law, Jesus holds, must be obeyed till the end of time. But there are two ways of obeying the Law: the way of the Pharisees and the teachers of the Law, and the way of my followers. The way of my followers, Jesus says, is a way of obeying the Law that surpasses that of the Pharisee and the teachers of the Law. It is a higher righteousness. Without this higher righteousness no one can enter the kingdom of God (5:20).

Only those who follow Jesus can have this higher righteousness. In fact, Jesus himself is this higher righteousness. For he is the only one who fulfills the Law down to its last detail. Jesus himself is the advantage his followers have over the Pharisees and the teachers of the Law. Jesus himself comes between his followers and the Law. Between the disciples and the Law stands Jesus, who perfectly fulfills the Law. The followers of Jesus face not a Law that has never been fulfilled but a Law whose demands Jesus has already satisfied. The righteousness demanded by the Law is already available. It is the righteousness of Jesus. By calling people to follow him, Jesus gives them his righteousness. "Of course, the righteousness of the disciples can never be a personal achievement; it is always a gift, which they received when they were called to follow him. In fact their righteousness consists precisely in their following him. . . , it is the visible righteousness of those who for the sake of Jesus are the light of the world and the city set on the hill. This is where the righteousness of the disciple exceeds that of the Pharisees; it is grounded solely upon the call to fellowship with him who alone fulfills the Law" (Dietrich Bonhoeffer, *The Cost of Discipleship*, London: SCM Press, 1959, pp. 113-114).

Six Examples

In Matthew 5:21-48, Jesus gives six examples of the "higher righteousness." In each example Jesus contrasts what God said long ago to Israel at Mount Sinai with what he himself says to his followers. Six times he quotes what the Law demands and six times he states what he demands:

The Law Says	But Jesus Says
1. Do not murder	1. Do not be angry
2. Do not commit adultery	2. Do not lust
3. Divorce on condition	3. Do not divorce
4. Keep the oaths you swore to God	4. Do not swear at all
5. Eye for eye, tooth for tooth	5. Do not resist an evil person
6. Love your neighbor, hate your enemy	6. Love your enemies

1. Murder (Matt. 5:21-26)

Murder under the Sinai Law is punishable by death: "Anyone who strikes a man and kills him shall surely be put to death" (Ex. 21:12). But Jesus says that not merely the outward act of murder but also the inward passion of anger exposes a person to God's judgment: "All acts of anger and injustice toward one's brother are, for the true disciple, equally serious, and are as grave as murder" (John P. Meier, *The Vision of Matthew*, p. 245).

2. Adultery (Matt. 5:27-30)

The Law says, You shall not commit adultery. Jesus radicalizes this commandment by forbidding lustful looks and thoughts. By doing so Jesus goes against tendency current in his day to fault the women. Jesus, instead, places the responsibility on those men guilty of lustful desires and glances. He is protecting the dignity of woman which men violate in the privacy of their thoughts and looks. My followers must be so deeply committed to both inward and outward moral purity, Jesus is saying, that rather than risk the punishment of hell they are willing to suffer the loss of their right hand or eye.

Marriage as Discipleship

"To enter sincerely into such a [marriage] vow, the Christian must first have committed himself or herself to God, and the commitment to the marriage partner grows out of that prior dedication. The very act of getting married is understood as an act of discipleship. The Christian marital relation, then, is modeled upon Christ's love for his church. Husband and wife are to love each other as Christ has loved them. That has always been the nature of Christian discipleship—the thankful response to God's act toward us in Jesus Christ, in a life of serving and caring patterned after the life of Christ."

—Elizabeth Achtemeier, *The Committed Marriage*, Philadelphia: Westminster Press, 1976, p. 102ff.

3. Divorce (Matt. 5:31-32)

The Law in Leviticus 18:6-18 forbids sexual relations with close relatives. It sets the limits within which a man may seek a wife. Generally speaking, these limits did not prevail in other parts of the Middle East where people did marry close relatives. As a result, the Law created serious problems for the church when it spread into the Gentile world. We read about one of these problems in 1 Corinthians 5:1, where Paul writes, "It is actually reported that there is sexual immorality [Greek: *porneia*] among you, and of a kind that does not occur even among pagans: A man has his father's wife." The expression "father's wife" refers to one's stepmother in Leviticus 18:8, so the precise relationship Paul is addressing seems to be a case of marriage with one's stepmother, a marriage forbidden in Leviticus 18:8. Remember that the church for which Matthew writes his gospel is a Jewish-Gentile church. It must repeatedly have faced the problem of Gentile converts whose marriages are forbidden by Leviticus 18. Could such converts retain their wives? Or should they divorce them? But what about the command of Jesus himself forbidding divorce? To solve this problem, claims John P. Meier, Matthew's church

> put into Jesus' prohibition of divorce [in Matthew 5:32] the clarification that this prohibition was not to be used to countenance an incestuous marriage contracted before a convert's baptism. The reply of the church was: true, Jesus forbade a man to dismiss his wife. But this prohibition does not apply in the case of an incestuous union . . . for that is not a true union, being forbidden by Leviticus 18. To use later terminology and distinctions not worked out in Matthew's day: the incestuous union was null and void from the beginning, and so did not fall under the Lord's prohibition of divorce, which was concerned with genuine marriages.

—*The Vision of Matthew*, pp. 254-255.

Jesus' words, "anyone who divorces his wife except for marital unfaithfulness [Greek: *porneias*]," rather than watering down an otherwise strict moral command in the face of practical necessity, rejects any compromising position on the question of converts entering the church with marriages that violate the law in Leviticus 18.

4. Oaths (Matt. 5:33-37)

The Law views oaths positively and in certain cases even imposes them. For example, when a woman is suspected of adultery a priest "shall put the woman under oath" (Num. 5:19). People must take oaths because they are habitual liars. But Jesus categorically prohibits oaths: "Do not swear at all," he says, because he expects his followers to be truthful of heart and lips. Jesus finds oaths objectionable. Oaths infringe on God's sovereignty, they drag God down into petty human affairs, they seek to make God the guarantor of human words.

5. Eye for Eye (Matt. 5:38-42)

The law of retaliation is clearly spelled out in Exodus 21:24, Leviticus 24:20, and Deuteronomy 19:21: eye for eye, tooth for tooth, hand for hand, foot for foot, burning for burning, wound for wound, stripe for stripe. Jesus categorically rejects this law for his followers. Retaliation produces bitterness and ill feelings. It multiplies evil. It poisons communities. It destroys rather than builds.

> **Revenge**
>
> "The only way to overcome evil is to let it run itself to a standstill because it does not find the resistance it is looking for. Resistance merely creates further evil and adds fuel to the flames. But when evil meets no opposition and encounters no obstacle but only patient endurance, its sting is drawn, and at last it meets an opponent which is more than its match."
>
> —Dietrich Bonhoeffer, *The Cost of Discipleship*, London: SCM Press, 1959, p. 127.

6. Love for Enemies (Matt. 5:43-48)

The higher righteousness culminates in Jesus' command to love even one's enemies. When people love their enemies, they love the way God loves. As the Father loves extravagantly, so must his children. As the Father shows mercy without end, so must his children. People will know Jesus' followers by their love.

In these six examples Jesus contrasts what God said to Israel of old at Mount Sinai with what he himself says to his followers now.

Following Luke's Jesus

What is unique about Luke's Jesus is the emphasis he places on prayer and discipleship. Before choosing twelve disciples, Jesus spends a night praying to God (Luke 6:12-13). Luke softens the picture of Peter's denial of Jesus by recording that Jesus offers intercessory prayer for Peter and then appoints him to strengthen the other disciples: "Simon, Simon, Satan has asked to sift you as wheat. But I have prayed for you [singular], that your faith may not fail. And when you have turned back, strengthen your brothers" (22:31-32). Also, right before telling his disciples the parable of the persistent widow, Jesus urges "that they should always pray and not give up" (18:1). Again, when Jesus sends out the seventy-two disciples (a story recorded only in Luke), he instructs them not only to heal the sick and to preach that the kingdom of God is near, but also to ask the Lord of the harvest "to send out workers in his harvest field" (10:2). And then, in the next chapter, Jesus teaches his disciples to pray the "Lord's Prayer" (11:2-4) and talks to them about the power of prayer (11:9-13). Jesus tells the disciples that God will give the Holy Spirit to those who ask and that this Spirit will energize the life of discipleship.

Following John's Jesus

In the gospel of John, Jesus' public ministry ends at chapter 12. In chapters 13 through 17 Jesus is alone with his disciples. The crowds are gone; the enemies are gone. Jesus talks exclusively to his followers, preparing them for discipleship after his departure. He talks about a variety of matters.

1. *Footwashing* (13:1-17). By washing the disciples' feet, Jesus becomes an example of humility and service. His servant behavior must guide their discipleship. As their master has treated them, so they must treat each other.

2. *Love* (13:34-35). Jesus issues a new command: the disciples should love one another as he has loved them. Their mutual love will tell the unbelieving world that they are disciples of Jesus.

3. *The Holy Spirit* (14:15-26). Jesus assures his disciples that during his absence they will not be deprived of God's presence. That presence is the Holy Spirit. Jesus promises the disciples that the Holy Spirit will reside with them forever and "will teach you all things and will remind you of everything I have said to you" (14:26). In the midst of changing times and different cultures, the Holy Spirit keeps Jesus' words alive.

4. *Peace* (14:27). The disciples need not fear Jesus' departure and absence, for he gives them his peace as a farewell present. His peace will keep their hearts from fear and confusion.

5. *Vine and Branches* (15:1-8). The disciples must reside in Jesus like branches reside in the vine. As long as they do, they will bear fruit. When they do not remain in Jesus, they will be sheared off the vine and cast into the fire. Residing in Jesus means allowing Jesus' words to reside in you (15:7).

6. *Hatred of the World* (15:18-25). Followers of Jesus must expect to be hated by the unbelieving world. They are, after all, not greater than their master. If the world hated Jesus, they will also hate his followers.

7. *Unity* (17:20-23). Jesus asks the Father that his disciples and all who believe in him through their message may be one, as he and the Father are one, and that their unity may lead the world to believe that the Father has sent Jesus.

Mark's Jesus, Matthew's Jesus, Luke's Jesus, and John's Jesus: these are not four, but one. But as a single ray of light passing through a prism refracts into a variety of colors, so Jesus' call to discipleship passing through the first-century Middle Eastern world refracts into a multiplicity of demands.

USING APOCALYPTIC LANGUAGE

What Is an Apocalypse?

M any people recognize the word *apocalypse* from contemporary book or movie titles. But the word and its associations are, of course, found in the Bible as well, and in this chapter we will study their place in the gospels.

The word *apocalypse* has a wild ring to it. It suggests history running out of control—the end of the world. "When you aren't sure whether it is bombs or stars that are falling out of the sky," says Eugene Peterson, "and people are rushing toward the cliffs like a herd of pigs, the scene is 'apocalyptic'" (*The Contemplative Pastor,* Carol Stream, Ill.: Word Publishing, 1989, p. 49). To describe apocalyptic scenes, we need special language—wild language.

Apocalyptic language is mysterious and veiled. It abounds in beasts, strange events, and supernatural beings. It's cosmic, not historical. Because apocalyptic language is so unlike everyday language, it's hard to understand.

In the Jewish world apocalyptic literature flourished between the second century B.C. and the first century A.D. This literature used apocalyptic language to describe what would happen in the future. Commonly, apocalyptists were deterministic—everything that happens, they said, has been foreseen in advance and has been recorded in God's books. And they were pessimistic about history—the evils at work in this world, they said, are so demonic and cosmic in scope that nothing short of a divine intervention can overcome them. Nothing can be done to improve the world. All that remains is to wait for God's intervention at the end of history. Apocalyptists held that the present age is hurrying toward an "Armageddon"—a great destruction—when they expected the momentary and cataclysmic end of the world and the dawn of a new age.

The New Testament also uses apocalyptic language. Although it proclaims a single message, the New Testament uses a variety of languages. It speaks, for example, historical language, creedal language, theological language, doxological language—and also apocalyptic language. Mark 13 and the book of Revelation, for example, use apocalyptic language. Still, they are not typical specimens of apocalyptic literature; their focus is different.

The apocalyptists' worldview differed radically from that of the early Christians who saw history not as meaningless but as invaded and conquered by Jesus Christ. True, like Jewish apocalyptists, the early Christians looked forward to the end. But they saw the end as the consummation of what God had already accomplished in Jesus' death and resurrection. Therefore, before looking forward, they looked backward: "The early Christians concentrated on the gospel, the message of what God in Christ had done for man's salvation. They were not unmindful, of course, of the future. They looked for the Christ to come as Judge. But even then they did not forget the cross. It was the same Christ that had been crucified who would be the Judge, and it was He whom they preached" (Leon Morris, *Apocalyptic*, p. 84). To Christians, then, the truly central thing was not the last judgment but the cross.

Mark 13, because of its apocalyptic imagery, is often called "the Little Apocalypse." But actually, many themes nor-

---

Alien to Our Age

"Surely there is no part of New Testament faith more alien to our age than this doctrine of a second coming. . . . Partly, I suppose, it is alien because of the grotesque, Hebraic images it is clothed in. Partly too, I suppose, it is alien to us because we have come to associate it so closely with the lunatic fringe—the millennial sects climbing to the tops of hills in their white robes to wait for the end of the world that never comes, knocking at the backdoor to hand out their tracts and ask if we have been washed in the blood of the lamb. But beneath the language that they are written in and the cranks that they have produced, if cranks they are, I suspect that what our age finds most alien in these prophecies of a second coming, a final judgment and redemption of the world, is their passionate hopefulness. . . . For people like us, the reasonably thoughtful, reasonably reasonable and realistic people like us, this apocalyptic hope for the more than possible is too hopeful. We cannot hope such a fantastic hope any more, at least not quite, not often."

—Frederick Buechner, *The Hungering Dark*, New York: Seabury Press, 1969, p. 119ff.

mally found in first-century apocalyptic writings are missing. For example, basic apocalyptic themes such as the holy war, the annihilation of Rome, the gathering of all dispersed Jews, the renewal of Jerusalem as the capital, and rule over the Gentiles—all are missing. Mark 13 is more a clarion call to discipleship than a typical example of apocalyptic speculation about the end of the world.

In this chapter we first will take a close look at Mark 13, then study its parallels in Matthew and Luke, and finally look at the way the gospel of John deals with apocalyptic events.

Mark 13

In the two chapters that precede Mark 13, tension between Jesus and the religious authorities is gradually mounting. A clash appears unavoidable. And when Jesus drives the merchants out of the temple, the chief priests and the teachers of the law begin looking for a way to kill him.

As Jesus leaves the temple, one of his disciples remarks, "Look, Teacher! What massive stones! What magnificent buildings!" (13:1). Magnificent indeed, for nothing in the landscape of Jesus' day matches the temple's splendor. Yet this temple, with its power and prestige, represents the most formidable resistance to Jesus' ministry. And Jesus pronounces a curse on the temple: "Not one stone here will be left on another; everyone will be thrown down." The surprised disciples ask, "Tell us, when will these things happen?" This question leads to the long discourse in Mark 13:5-37, followed at once in Mark 14-15 by the passion story.

Jesus' discourse in chapter 13 and the events of chapters 14-15 appear at first glance to have little continuity. But a careful reading reveals that the two sections are actually closely linked. For, as we shall see, despite the use of apocalyptic language, the focus of Mark 13 is not on the end of time but on following Jesus into suffering and death. The following comparison of certain passages in Mark 13 and in Mark 14-15 reveals how Jesus' discourse provides a lens for viewing the earth-shaking events to follow.

1. *You will be handed over.* Jesus warns his disciples that they "will be handed over to the local councils and flogged in the synagogues. On account of me you will stand before governors and kings as witnesses to them" (13:9). Jesus' disciples will be handed over; in Mark 14-15, Jesus himself is handed over to the Jewish and Roman courts. His disciples will be flogged; Jesus himself is beaten by both Jewish and Roman court attendants (14:65; 15:19). His disciples will have to give testimony before governors and kings; Jesus himself testifies before Pilate that he is the king of the Jews (15:2). The disciples will witness that "brother will betray brother to death" (13:12); Jesus is betrayed by one of his own disciples.

2. *The coming of the Son of Man.* In Mark 13:26 Jesus promises that the Son of Man will be coming in clouds with great power and glory. This promise recalls his words to the Sanhedrin in Mark 14:62, where Jesus identifies himself with the Son of Man and says to the high priest, "And you will see the Son of Man sitting at the right hand of the Mighty One and coming on the clouds of heaven."

3. *Stand firm to the end.* In Mark 13:13 Jesus warns his disciples that "all men will hate you because of me, but he who stands firm to the end will be saved." But already in the next chapter, in Mark 14, none of the disciples stands firm. Judas betrays Jesus, Peter denies him, and all desert Jesus and flee.

4. *The sun will be darkened.* In Mark 13:24-25 Jesus says that, as a prelude to his coming as the Son of Man on the clouds of heaven, "the sun will be darkened and the moon will not give its light; the stars will fall from the sky, and the heavenly bodies will be shaken." Here Jesus is using the language of Old Testament prophets: "The sun and the moon are darkened, and the stars no longer shine" (Joel 2:10), and "The rising sun will be darkened and the moon will not give its light" (Isa. 13:10).

    In other words, in Mark 13:24-25 Jesus is using familiar Jewish vocabulary. Rather than talking cosmology, he is talking theology. He's not talking about the meltdown of the universe; he is using typical Jewish imagery to describe events that are earth-shaking and that lead history to its appointed climax. What climax? Jesus' crucifixion—when the sun is darkened, when from noon till three "darkness came over the whole land" (15:33).

5. *The hour has come.* In Mark 13:32-33 Jesus tells his disciples that no one knows the hour of his return, "not even the angels in heaven, nor the

Son, but only the Father. Be on guard! Be alert!" Compare this warning with the scene in Gethsemane. Jesus asks Peter, James, and John to watch and pray with him. He himself then goes a little farther and prays that if possible the hour might pass from him. "Abba, Father," he prays, "everything is possible for you. Take this cup from me. Yet not what I will, but what you will" (14:36). The divinely appointed hour still has not arrived. Meanwhile, the three disciples whom Jesus has warned in Mark 13 to be alert and on guard while awaiting the hour of his coming as the Son of Man, are already going to sleep in Mark 14. This draws Jesus' rebuke: "Are you still sleeping and resting? Enough! The hour has come. Look, the Son of Man is betrayed into the hands of sinners" (14:41).

6. *Sudden return.* Jesus' discourse in Mark 13 concludes with a short parable about a master and his slaves. The parable warns against the danger of falling asleep. Jesus says to keep watch "because you do not know when the owner of the house will come back—whether in the evening, or at midnight, or when the rooster crows, or at dawn" (13:35). These specific times of day also create links to Jesus' passion. Mark 14 records: when *evening* came, Jesus told his disciples that one of them would betray him; in Gethsemane when Jesus came to his disciples *at midnight,* he found them sleeping; after Peter disowned Jesus *the rooster crowed.* And Mark 15 opens by saying that "very early in the morning," at dawn, Jesus was led away to his trial and death. In other words, the disciples whom Jesus warns to be alert in Mark 13 are already betraying him and going to sleep on him and denying him in Mark 14. Jesus' concluding words in Mark 13:35-37 sum up the main point Mark wishes to make: "Watch!"

Clearly then, Mark 13 is a preface to the passion story. Before Mark 13 looks forward to the end, it looks backward to the cross. Mark 13 is first of all about Jesus' trial and death. In contemporary apocalyptic language it tells how to view these climactic events. It calls us to discipleship in a world that has no room for Jesus and his followers, for Jesus' followers may not expect a fate different from their crucified Lord's. They must expect to be hated and per-

History Has But One Theme

"World history has only one theme: the manifestation of the glory of Jesus Christ. More and more world history must be unmasked; its potentialities must be exhausted, till men see what happens when they are left to themselves, and how terrible is the end of all human possibilities."

—Hanns Lilje, *The Last Book of the Bible,* Philadelphia: Fortress Press, 1957, p. 23.

secuted for being Jesus' followers. They must constantly remind themselves that only those who stand firm to the end will be saved (13:13).

Matthew's Version of Mark 13

Matthew by and large incorporates all of Mark 13 into his version of Jesus' apocalyptic discourse. Matthew, however, adds three kinds of new material:

1. *Two warnings against false prophets (Matt. 24:11-13, 26-28).* By adding two more warnings to Mark's single warning, Matthew highlights the role of false prophets at the beginning (24:5), toward the center (24:11-13), and near the climax (24:26-28) of Jesus' discourse. So Matthew's Jesus sees false prophets threatening his followers everywhere. These prophets are especially dangerous because they attack the church from within, claiming to possess inside knowledge about the presence of Christ. They claim, for example, that Christ is "out in the desert" or "in the inner rooms" (24:26)—places not easily accessible to the average Christian. By claiming to have information that other Christians lack and by performing "great signs and miracles" (24:24), they deceive many (24:5) and turn many away from the faith (24:10). Matthew's Jesus sternly warns against these successful and extraordinary Christians. He calls them *false* prophets because they do the things Deuteronomy 13:1-3 warns against: "If a prophet, or one who foretells by dreams, appears among you and announces to you a miraculous sign or wonder, and if the sign or wonder of which he has spoken takes place, and he says, 'Let us follow other gods' (gods you have not known) and 'let us worship them,' you must not listen to the words of that prophet or dreamer. The Lord your God is testing you to find out whether you love him with all your heart and with all your soul."

2. *Parabolic sayings (Matt. 24:37-44).* Jesus, the Son of Man, will return. His return is implied in his resurrection, and Jesus' disciples must be prepared. Unlike the careless people in Noah's day or a homeowner who does not watch against robbers, Christians should be ready. Their living

must be radically directed to the coming of the Son of Man. They must be watchful.

3. *Three parables.* The same theme of watchfulness also runs through the parables in Matthew 24:45-25:30. In the parable of the faithful and wise servant (24:45-51) the way to be watching for the return of the master is to be faithful in feeding the members of the master's household. The focus of attention must be the table, not the sky. The second parable, the parable of the ten virgins (25:1-13), ends with the warning, "Therefore keep watch, because you do not know the day or the hour." The return of Christ is not datable. It may be more distant than we anticipate. It may require a supply of oil we think is an unwise investment. The third parable, the parable of the talents (25:14-30), comes down very hard on the servant to whom the master has entrusted only one talent. Why is this servant singled out? Because he uses his lack of more talents as an excuse for doing nothing. He lives by the mistaken notion that what he does is too insignificant to invite his master's negative judgment.

> **Second Coming Versus Progress**
>
> "The doctrine of the Second Coming is deeply uncongenial to the whole evolutionary or developmental character of modern thought. We have been taught to think of the world as something that grows slowly towards perfection, something that 'progresses' or 'evolves.' Christian Apocalyptic offers us no such hope. It does not even foretell . . . a gradual decay. It foretells a sudden, violent end imposed from without; an extinguisher popped onto the candle, a brick flung at the gramophone, a curtain rung down on the play—'Halt!'"
>
> —C. S. Lewis, *The World's Last Night and Other Essays*, New York: Harcourt, Brace & World, 1960, p. 100ff.

In each of these three parables, Christ's return and judgment coincide. The return is for judgment. Therefore keep watch!

Luke's Version of Mark 13

When Luke wrote chapter 21:5-38 he obviously had Mark 13 in front of him. Much of Luke has parallels in Mark 13. But being a writer and not a copier, Luke shaped the material to reflect his own perspective. To understand this perspective, we must recall that Luke not only wrote a gospel but also the book of Acts. Acts continues where the Gospel of Luke leaves off. When Luke writes, "In my former book, Theophilus, I wrote about all that Jesus began to do and to teach" (Acts 1:1), he refers to the gospel he has already written. This one work Luke-Acts has a common theme: Jesus inaugurates a worldwide community in which the distinction between Jew and Gentile is obsolete. This theme is apparent, for example, in the way Luke and Acts both begin and end. Luke's gospel begins with Simeon describing Jesus as "a light for revelation to the Gentiles" (2:32) and ends with Jesus charging his disciples to preach repentance and forgiveness of sins in his name "to all nations" (24:27). Acts begins with the disciples preaching to "God-fearing Jews from every nation under heaven" (2:5) and ends with Paul preaching this message in Rome: "God's salvation has been sent to the Gentiles" (28:28). There can be no question, writes W. D. Davies, "that for Luke the greatest fact of the first century was the church in which the division between Jew and Gentile had been annulled" (*Invitation to the New Testament,* p. 224). But thinking in terms of evangelizing the Gentile world implies that the expectation of the imminent end of all things cannot dominate Luke. The end *will* come soon, but planting of churches throughout the Roman provinces requires a longer stay in this world.

Turning to Luke's version of Mark 13, we can see how Luke's focus on the task of worldwide witness has led to a shift in emphasis in Jesus' discourse. The Son of Man *will* come in a cloud with power and great glory (21:24). But *only* when "the times of the Gentiles are fulfilled" (21:24), when the signs appear in the sun, moon, and stars (21:25), and when the nations are "in anguish and perplexity at the roaring and tossing of the sea" (21:25) and "faint from terror, apprehensive of what is coming on the world" (21:26). Luke presents the following time frame:

- First the period of persecution (21:12-19),
- then the period of political distress and dissolution (21:20-24),
- then the fulfillment of the times of the Gentiles (21:24),
- then the period of cosmic signs and dissolution (21:25-26),
- then the coming of the Son of Man (21:27).

Both Mark and Luke think of the events preceding the coming of the Son of Man as closely pressed together in time, but Luke also thinks in terms of a brief interim granted by God to allow for the gospel proclamation to the Gentiles. Accordingly, Luke omits the theme of the Lord mercifully cutting short those days of suffering (Mark 13:20). In short, in Luke the imminence of the end is not the sole dominating factor. The worldwide proclamation of the gospel enters into the time scheme as well. The evangelizing church needs a brief period of time in which to carry out its mission mandate.

Apocalypse Now

We have looked at Mark 13 and its parallel passages in both Mathew and Luke. When next we look for a comparable apocalyptic passage in the gospel of John, we discover that there isn't any. John does indeed contain passages speaking of future apocalyptic events, but these events are not central to John's total scheme of things. Clearly, a shift of perspective has taken place between Mark and John. In Mark and Matthew and Luke the future is of utmost importance; in John end-time events such as the coming of Christ, the resurrection, and the judgment belong much more to the here and now.

The Coming of Christ

Although John does not deny the second coming of Christ, he focuses on the first coming instead. In the gospel of Mark, at the end of Jesus' ministry, the high priest demands to know his identity: "Are you the Christ, the Son of the Blessed One?" (14:61). Jesus' answer is, "I am. And you will see the Son of Man sitting at the right hand of the Mighty One and coming on the clouds of heaven." In the gospel of John, however, a similar statement appears at the beginning of Jesus' ministry: "You shall see heaven open, and the angels of God ascending and descending on the Son of Man" (1:51). To understand the significance of these words in John we must be aware of the fundamental difference between John and the other three gospels: John's Jesus is someone who repeatedly speaks of a previous life with God before he came down to earth. In John, the all-important coming down from heaven takes place *before* Jesus' public ministry rather than at the end of time, as in

If Christ Is Coming Again

"If the Lord is coming again, if all the floods and fires that cleanse the world will subside before his throne, if at the Last Day those who have been saved need not look back into a world-wide grave wherein lie buried . . . also their ideas of God and their dreams of a heavenly Father, if instead they are able to sing, 'God has brought us to this place'— I say, if all that is so, then the present moment of my life is also radically changed. Then my death is not merely a departure, but a going home. Then war and terror, plane crashes and mine disasters, marital difficulties and stays in the hospital are no longer simply impersonal results of natural processes; they cease to be 'visitations' and become 'visits.' Someone is there. His heart is both the source and the goal of it all."

—Helmut Thielicke, *How Modern Should Theology Be?* Philadelphia: Fortress Press, 1969, p. 68.

the first three gospels. In John, the Jesus standing before the disciples is the descended Son of Man on whom the angels of God wait. What in the first three gospels is future expectation, in John is present reality.

Judgment

In John, apart from a few texts on the last judgment (5:29-29; 6:39-40, 44-54; 12:48), judgment falls here and now, upon the hearing of Jesus' words. The words of Jesus themselves judge all who hear but do not believe (12:48). The Greek word for judgment is *krisis*, from which we derive the English word *crisis*. Hearing Jesus' words places people in a crisis of having to choose for or against him. Those who accept his words are not condemned, but those who do not accept them stand condemned already because they have "not believed in the name of God's one and only Son" (3:18).

Resurrection

In John 6:40 Jesus says that at the last day he will raise up everyone who believes in him, but in John resurrection can also take place here and now, for resurrection is the experience of being brought to belief in Christ. In the story of Lazarus in John 11, for example, in response to Mary's belief that her deceased brother Lazarus "will rise again in the resurrection at the last day" (11:24), Jesus posits: "I am the resurrection and the life. He who believes in me will live, even though he dies; and whoever lives and believes in me will never die." In other words, for those who believe in Christ resurrection is an experience in this life.

John's emphasis on present rather than on future apocalyptic events stems from his conviction that God's future gifts are even now partly available. John's message to the late first-century Christians who experienced disappointment at the delay of the second coming of Christ is this: Stop focusing so much attention on the future. Stop your excessive longing for the return of Christ. The salvation God has promised is accessible to believers now. In a real sense, apocalypse is now. After all, the Counselor or Holy Spirit has taken the place of Jesus. He is another Jesus. He substitutes for Jesus. Just as Jesus spoke nothing of his own but only what he had heard from the Father (8:28; 12:49), so the Counselor speaks nothing of his own but only what he hears from Jesus (16:13). What Jesus is to the Father, the Counselor is to Jesus. Jesus may not yet have returned as we expected, John is saying, but in a very real sense he has already returned in and through the Counselor.

SESSION 10

CREATING SPACE
FOR THE GENTILES

E ach of the four gospels contains stories of conflict between Jesus and the religious leaders of his people. Lurking behind these conflicts is the temple and the whole system of temple worship. The very first conflict story in Mark is set against the unspoken background of temple worship. The scene is a house in Capernaum. Four carriers lower a paralytic through an opening in the roof above Jesus. When Jesus sees their faith he says to the paralytic, "Son, your sins are forgiven" (Mark 2:5). Hearing this, some teachers of the law think to themselves, This man is blaspheming! After all, who can forgive sins but God alone? The teachers of the law claim that God forgives sins on the basis of sacrifices commanded in the book of Leviticus and through ordained priests. God forgives only through temple sacrifices and temple priests. Anyone who thinks that sins can be forgiven independently of the temple undermines its position. So when Jesus claims to have power from God to forgive sins, he is challenging the temple. And Jesus' words addressed to the paralytic are a direct blow to the temple's monopoly to forgive sins on God's behalf. This first conflict in Mark also foreshadows Jesus' ultimate conflict with the temple as recorded by all four gospels in the story of the clearing of the temple.

An Angry Christ

"What are we to make of this outburst, this account of an angry Christ? Did Jesus slip out of character here? Did He 'lose his temper,' as we express it, to become more human than divine? Does it reveal an impetuosity in Him which, had He lived longer, He would have learned to curb? Or is there, perhaps, a confusion in our minds as to the real character of His divine nature? Was Jesus less divine here, with the whip in His hands, than when He stretched those hands on a cross to take the nails? How the questions swarm about this picture, and about others in the Gospels in which He is presented as a man blazing with anger!"

—J. Wallace Hamilton, *Ride the Wild Horses!* Westwood, NJ: Fleming H. Revell Co., 1952, p. 114ff.

This temple story has been the focal point of much discussion in recent decades. Nearly all recent books about Jesus devote space to it. Most scholars agree on two basic matters: (1) Jesus chooses the temple as the place for his most dramatic public action; and (2) Jesus' action is a major reason for his execution. But here agreement tends to stop and questions begin: What exactly is it that Jesus did? Why did he do it? In what way was his action the cause of his death? Three basic answers have been given to these questions. We will consider each of them.

Answer One: Jesus Purifies the Temple

The older and still widely held understanding of the event is that Jesus is acting as a reformer. Seeing all the business transacted in the temple, Jesus becomes incensed and purges the temple precincts. As he purifies the temple, clearing the outer court of traders, their animals, and money changers, he justifies what he is doing by quoting Isaiah and Jeremiah. Jesus' purpose is to restore a worshipful atmosphere. He accuses the people of having turned the temple into a place where making profit is the number one interest. He accuses the priests of misusing their calling by engaging in business.

Critique

In this interpretation of Jesus' action in the temple, the focus is doing business—the changing of money and the selling of animals. Jesus then is distinguishing between the true purpose of the temple—a purpose he wholeheartedly approves of—and the abusive practices that detract from it. By purifying the temple, this argument goes, Jesus is symbolically condemning these practices and the priests who are responsible for them. And he is calling the temple authorities back to the true purpose of the temple.

The weakness of this interpretation lies in assuming that Jesus is making a distinction between abusive practices and the real purpose of the temple. For if we say that Jesus intends to return the temple to the pure worship of God, aren't we forgetting the basic function of the temple? The temple, according to God's command, was the place of sacrifice. And according to God's command, these sacrifices required unblemished animals. But where could people obtain the animals? In the time of Jesus, explains biblical scholar E. P. Sanders, "the temple had long been the only place in Israel at which sacrifices could be offered, and this means that suitable animals and birds must have been in supply at the temple site. There was not an 'original' time when worship at the temple had been 'pure' from the business which the requirement of unblemished sacrifices creates" (*Jesus and Judaism*, p. 63). So long as people could remember, temple worship had always involved buying sacrificial animals and having them inspected to make sure they were "without defect" (Lev. 1:3). For how would temple worship continue if trading in animals were to cease? Sacrifice was the principal act in Jewish worship and was so by divine command.

And changing money into temple currency was also necessary to keep the temple functioning. The money that pilgrims brought with them had to be changed into coins that did not have the image of a king or emperor imprinted on them. Pilgrims used the temple coins to purchase sacrificial animals and to pay the half-shekel annual temple tax levied on all Jews. This changing of money can hardly be seen as an abuse, unless, of course, the money changers charged fat commissions or bribed the priests. But evidence of these types of abuse is altogether missing from the gospel accounts. The most important point to recognize here, Sanders reminds us, "is that the requirement to present an *unblemished* dove as a sacrifice for certain impurities or transgressions was a requirement *given by God to Israel through Moses*. The business arrangements around the temple were necessary if the commandments were to be obeyed" (*Jesus and Judaism*, p. 65). Thus answer one does not provide a satisfactory explanation of Jesus' action in the temple.

Answer Two: Jesus Creates Space for Gentiles

A more promising way of dealing with Jesus' action in the temple is to ask, How does Jesus himself interpret what he is doing? The answer is by quoting Old Testament prophets. In Mark 11:17, Jesus quotes these words from Isaiah 56:7, "My house will be called a house of prayer for all nations." What is at stake in the clearing of the temple, he is saying, is the status of the Gentiles because the trade was being conducted in the so-called court of the Gentiles. By clearing this area and by reciting from Isaiah 56, Jesus indicates that he is concerned about what has happened to the role of Gentiles in the worship of Israel's God.

The passage Jesus cites from the Old Testament is Isaiah 56:3-8, a passage speaking of end-time promises and describing those who will be included in God's people. The prophet singles out eunuchs and foreigners. Both had been victims of discrimination and shut out from God's people. Isaiah 56 asks a community, Who is in and who is out? Who is acceptable to Israel's God and who is not? Who is fit to worship God in his temple and who is not? And the anticipated answer is, Certainly not the eunuchs, for they are physically blemished. And certainly not the foreigners, for they are racially blemished. Isaiah 56, which dates from the period following the Babylonian exile, addresses a Jewish community that is narrowly nationalistic. Somewhere along the way, it seems, the Jewish people had lost sight of the fact that God had chosen them to be "a light for the Gentiles" (Isa. 42:6). Isaiah 56 reminds them of their missionary calling. The temple, it says, is not just for Jews; it's a house of prayer for all people. God will make joyful all "foreigners who bind themselves to the Lord, to serve him. . . . Their burnt offerings and sacrifices will be accepted on my altar; for my house will be called a house of prayer for all nations." Isaiah 56 counters the spirit of exclusiveness. It proclaims that a time will come when there no longer will be two classes of worshipers. Then Gentiles will be as fully privileged as Jewish people to offer sacrifices to Israel's God.

Jesus' action in the temple announces that the time of Jewish-Gentile worship *has arrived*. The time has arrived when people from every nation will say, "Come, let us go to the mountain of the Lord, to the house of the God of Jacob" (Isa. 2:3; Mic. 4:2). The Old Testament promise has become reality. Jesus' action in the temple is not concerned with clearing space for Gentiles in the outer court. Such an interpretation of Jesus' action implies that the Gentiles belong in the outer court, while Israel continues to enjoy a fuller worship within the inner courts. There is no suggestion of lesser status for Gentiles in Isaiah 56. Rather, this prophetic passage anticipates Gentiles having the *same* privileges as the Jews. It clearly refers to the sacrifices and offerings of the Gentiles as well as to their prayers. It does away with the distinction of first and second class worshipers. It universalizes the Jewish worship of God.

Answer Three: Jesus Symbolically Destroys the Temple

Isaiah 56:3-8, the passage from which Jesus quotes, is immediately followed by a passage that speaks critically of Israel's leaders and accuses them of being blind and lacking knowledge (56:10). This accusation provides a natural link to the phrase from Jeremiah 7:11 that Jesus quotes next. Jesus accuses the people he is teaching of having made the temple into "a den of robbers."

This phrase—"a den of robbers"—is found in Jeremiah's sermon denouncing the temple. The thrust of this sermon is that Israel's God has no need for the temple in Jerusalem any more than he had need for the sanctuary in Shiloh, which he allowed the Philistines to destroy. For the temple to survive similar destruction, Israel must obey. To press home this message, Jeremiah urges the people to go and visit Shiloh: "Go now to the place in Shiloh where I first made a dwelling place for my Name, and see what I did to it because of the wickedness of my people Israel" (7:12). Because the people "steal and murder, commit adultery and perjury," says Jeremiah, God will do to the temple what he did to the sanctuary in Shiloh. He will have it destroyed. The phrase "a den of robbers," therefore, suggests destruction.

> **What Might This Action Mean?**
>
> In Gerd Theissen's book *The Shadow of the Galilean* one of the characters answers the question about the meaning of Jesus' action in the temple as follows: "I've only suggestions. First, Jesus prevents workers carrying tools through the temple. That's a protest against the rebuilding of the temple. They've been working on it now for half a century and it still isn't finished. Perhaps Jesus is rejecting the building of this temple. Secondly, Jesus overthrows tables. Does he mean to say that the temple will be overthrown and will collapse in this way? Is he announcing a destruction of the temple? At all events I see this action as a blatant attack on the temple. Thirdly, he prevents money-changers and those who sell sacrificial animals from going about their business. The money which is changed is used to buy animals. Without these businesses there would be no sacrificial cult. So is Jesus against bloody sacrifices? What use is it if you don't sacrifice in it?"
>
> —Philadelphia: Fortress Press, 1987, p. 144ff.

Jesus' clearing of the outer court represents an attack on the temple worship itself, and symbolizes its destruction. Biblical scholar N. T. Wright explains, "Without the Temple-tax, the regular daily sacrifices could not be supplied. Without the right money, individual worshippers could not purchase their sacrificial animals. Without the animals, sacrifice could not be offered. Without sacrifice, the Temple has lost its whole *raison d'etre*" (*Jesus and the Victory of God,* p. 423). This interpretation of Jesus' action as a symbolic destruction of the temple is supported by its setting in Mark's gospel: the incident of the cursing and withering of the fig tree.

The fig tree incident. Mark places Jesus' clearing of the outer court smack in the center of the fig tree incident, between the cursing of the fig tree and its withering. In this way, Mark sheds light on the temple incident. Placing a story within a story is one of Mark's favorite literary techniques. Mark begins telling one story, interrupts it with another complete story, and then finishes telling the first story. Mark's technique invites the reader to see each story in the light of the other. In our example, in Mark 11, the two stories divide like this:

- Story one begins: Jesus curses the fig tree (Mark 11:12-14).
- Story two begins and ends: Jesus symbolically destroys the temple (11:15-19).
- Story one ends: The fig tree withers (11:20-21).

As the story begins, Jesus and his disciples are on the way from Bethany to Jerusalem when Jesus becomes hungry. Fortunately, he spots a fig tree—the kind that produces figs in the middle of the summer. Unfortunately, it's early spring. The fig tree has leaves but no figs. Then Jesus does the unexpected. He curses the tree: "May no one ever eat fruit from you again." But doesn't Jesus know that a fig tree can't produce figs out of season? Of course he does. Why then does he curse the tree? And why does Mark insert that embarrassing line, "because it was not the season for figs"? Why doesn't Mark leave it out (as Matthew does)? Because Mark wants his readers to notice that line and alert them that something more is at stake here than a mix-up of seasons. Mark wants his readers to say, "But that's unreasonable! No tree can be expected to produce fruit out of season." And then, once they say that, they are ready to understand Jesus' behavior in the temple. For, like the fig tree, the temple is not bearing fruit either. The temple is out of season and is intentionally and officially kept that way. The area where Gentiles *are* allowed is used for commercial purposes. It is this that infuriates Jesus, for it strikes at the heart of his mission. Jesus comes looking for fruit but finds that the temple is kept out of season, that the court of the Gentiles is kept barren of Gentiles. But the season of fig gathering is now, Jesus is saying. The season of joined Jewish-Gentile worship is now! Therefore, as he had destroyed the fig tree, Jesus now symbolically destroys the temple.

Matthew's Version of the Temple Story (Matt. 21:12-17)

Matthew's version differs from Mark's in four ways:

1. *Sequence of events.* In Mark, on the day of his triumphal entry into Jerusalem, Jesus visits the temple, looks around, and then returns to Bethany. He does not clear the temple until the next day. But Matthew changes Mark's order, placing the clearing on the same day as the triumphant entry. By shortening Mark's time span by one day Matthew is forced to compress the cursing and withering of the fig tree into a single, sudden event. Immediately after Jesus curses the tree it withers. Furthermore, in Matthew the fig tree incident serves an entirely different purpose than in Mark. In Mark, it foreshadows the destruction of the temple. In Matthew, it demonstrates the power of faith: "If you have faith and do not doubt, not only can you do what was done to the fig tree, but also you can say to this mountain, 'Go, throw yourself into the sea,' and it will be done" (21:21).

2. *"For all nations."* Though Matthew's Jesus quotes the words from Isaiah 56:7, "My house will be called a house of prayer," he omits the words, "for all nations." We must remember that Matthew wrote his gospel somewhere between A. D. 80 and 90, at least ten years after the destruction of Jerusalem. With the temple in ruins and with the calling to be an international house of prayer having been passed on to the Christian church, the shorter quote from Isaiah makes sense.

3. *The blind and the lame.* Matthew's Jesus heals the blind and the lame who come to him at the temple (21:14). Because they are physically blemished, blind and

---

Jesus Still Visits the Temple

"The Jesus who threw the traders out of the temple foretold that *that* temple would fall, so that one stone would not remain upon another. After it had fallen in fact, he came to St. John on Patmos, and, in the vision of Revelation, delivered judgment on the new temple which God had raised up in place of the old. For the gospel is everlasting. What Jesus does in the gospel he always does: he still visits, and purifies, the temple. He stands in our midst; and what does he find? Not cattle here, but cobwebs; and by which is his Father more dishonoured? By corruption, profanity, and noise; or by neglect, emptiness and disobedience?"

—Austin Farrer, *The Essential Sermons,* Cambridge, Mass.: Cowley Publications, 1991, p. 160.

lame people are barred from the temple. So when Jesus heals them he announces that the kingdom of God has come near. Remember John the Baptist's question earlier in the gospel, "Are you the one who was to come, or should we expect someone else?" (Matt. 11:3). Jesus' answer was, "Go back and report to John what you have heard and see: The blind receive sight, the lame walk." In this answer Jesus is quoting from Isaiah 35, where the dawning of the messianic age is said to be visible in the healing of the blind and the lame. Similarly, Jesus' healing miracles in the temple announce the dawn of the age of salvation.

4.   *Children.* In Matthew 21:15 the children in the temple area are shouting, "Hosanna to the Son of David." When the guardians of the temple take offense at this messianic title, Jesus accuses them of not knowing the scriptures well, for otherwise they would see in the children's acclamation the fulfillment of Psalm 8:3, "From the lips of children and infants you have ordained praise."

Luke's Version of the Temple Story (Luke 19:45-46)

Among the four gospel writers, Luke is the only one to view the temple positively. For him the temple *remains* the place of worship and prayer. This can be seen from the stories that are unique to Luke:

1.   A priest named Zechariah is on duty in the temple (1:8).

2.   Joseph and Mary fulfil their cultic duty by offering "a sacrifice in keeping with what is said in the law of the Lord: 'a pair of doves or two young pigeons'" (2:24).

3.   Simeon and the prophetess Anna who "never left the temple but worshiped night and day" (2:37) are waiting for "the consolation of Israel" (2:25) in the temple.

4.   Jesus at the age of twelve teaches the teachers of Israel in the temple (2:41-50). To his concerned parents he says, "Didn't you know I had to be in my Father's house?"

5. After Jesus' ascension the disciples are "continually at the temple prais-
    ing God" (24:53).

In view of this, writes theologian Fred B. Craddock, it is no surprise "that
Luke's account of the cleansing is the briefest of the four, for in Luke there is
no hint that what Jesus did was a blow announcing the end of the temple
and its services. He purifies it in order that it can be the place of his own
ministry of teaching" (*Luke,* Louisville: John Knox Press, 1990, p. 229). Thus
the two verses following the clearing of the temple (19:47-48) focus on the
teaching of Jesus in the temple and make the teaching, rather than the clearing of the temple, the reason why the temple guardians seek to destroy Jesus.
Luke's view of the temple might explain why he omits the entire fig tree incident and why he eliminates all the violent details and curtails his description
to "And he entered the temple and began to drive out those who sold."

John's Version of the Temple Story (John 2:12-22)

John's version of the temple story occurs at the beginning of his gospel.
The incident takes place immediately after Jesus' first miraculous sign at the
wedding in Cana of Galilee. A comparison of John's temple story with those
of the other gospels raises three questions:

1. *Once or twice?* Does John's Jesus clear the temple court once or twice? Is
    there one clearing or are there two clearings, one at the beginning and
    one at the end of Jesus' ministry? There are good reasons to believe that
    there is only one. Mark and John have too many Greek words in com-
    mon and share too many features to suggest two separate clearings.
    They both share such features as
    • temple courts
    • driving out the sellers of doves
    • overturning the tables of money changers
    • referring to the temple as a house

It is also highly unlikely that such a serious attack on the temple would have been permitted twice, just as, say, a second bomb attack on the World Trade Center in New York City is highly unlikely to occur.

2. *Here or there?* Assuming a single clearing, did it take place at the beginning or at the end of Jesus' ministry? On this point biblical scholars are about equally divided. Those who opt for John's dating of the event at the beginning of Jesus' ministry point out, for example, that "at the trial of Jesus his statement about the Temple is recalled with difficulty by the witnesses as if it had been uttered long before; in John's chronology it would have been uttered at least two years before" (Raymond E. Brown, *The Gospel according to John I-XII*, p. 117). They further point out that, according to the first three gospels, Jesus journeys to Jerusalem only once during his ministry, right before his death. With the temple being in Jerusalem, their writers had no other choice but to place the temple scene right before Jesus' arrest. In the gospel of John, on the other hand, Jesus journeys to Jerusalem on several occasions. This allows John to place the story at the beginning, when it supposedly happened. Scholars opting for a late date argue that Jesus' action would most certainly have forced the authorities into taking immediate action by arresting Jesus. So when did the clearing of the temple take place—at the beginning or at the end? To come up with a satisfactory answer we must turn to the next question and delve into John's theology.

3. *Why here?* If the clearing of the temple took place at the end, why did John place it at the threshold of Jesus' ministry? This question leads us to the prologue of John's gospel. Here we read that the Word became flesh in Jesus of Nazareth and that God's glory filled him. The Word, in other words, replaces the temple as the place where God's glory dwells on earth: "The Word became flesh and lived for a while among us. We have seen his glory, the glory of the one and only Son, who came from the Father, full of grace and truth" (1:14). At the time of the exodus from Egypt, the *tabernacle* served as the dwelling place of God among his people. On the day of its inauguration "the glory of the Lord filled the tabernacle" (Ex. 40:34), Centuries later, Solomon built God a new dwelling place, the temple. At its inauguration "the glory of the Lord filled his temple" (1 Kings 8:11). Ten centuries later, when the Word became flesh, God relocates his glory. God's glory fills Jesus of Nazareth. This makes the institution of the temple obsolete. Jesus replaces the temple, as he replaces all Jewish institutions. For example, at the wedding at Cana (John 2:1-11) Jesus replaces the Jewish rite of "ceremonial wash-

ing." Jesus changes the water set aside for purification into wine and by so doing "revealed his glory, and his disciples put their faith in him" (2:11). John calls the miracle a sign, for it signifies who Jesus is. It manifests his divine glory. It points forward to his death and resurrection when his full glory will be revealed. Water changed into wine signifies that with Jesus' coming the religion of the law (symbolized by water) is changed into the religion of the gospel (symbolized by wine). The wine signifies the blood Jesus will shed for the forgiveness of sins. The abundance of wine signifies the arrival of the messianic age when "new wine will drip from the mountains and flow from all the hills" (Amos 9:13).

Jesus also replaces the temple. John removes the temple story from the chronology of the other gospels and makes it the first public act of Jesus for theological reasons. In the other gospels the temple clearing is part of the passion story, helping to explain why Jesus was put to death. At the trial before the Sanhedrin false witnesses testify that Jesus threatened to destroy the temple and to rebuild it in three days (Mark 14:58; Matt. 26:61). Their testimony is a contributing cause of Jesus' death. John, however, is not concerned with historical causes of Jesus' death in his gospel. He is not interested in the temple clearing as a cause of Jesus' death. For in John, Jesus' death is not caused by anyone or anything. Jesus died when his divinely appointed "hour" had come. Only then did he lay down his life (10:17-18). Jesus' death is from above. Its hour is ordained by the Father. Thus John's placement of the temple story is determined, not by historical but by theological considerations. In John, Jesus' words about destroying and raising the temple (2:19) refer to his own body, crucified and raised, so that it was only after he was raised that his disciples recalled what he had said. Robert Kysar sums it up well: "The temple is the dwelling place of God on earth. It is the point in space where one can find God among his people. But John claims that with Jesus the point in space has been shifted from the physical temple in Jerusalem to the person of Jesus himself. Only the resurrection will make that clear, but John signals the message already in this passage" (John's Story of Jesus, p. 25).

Why is the temple story the focal point of so much discussion in recent decades? Because the story shows Jesus for what he truly is. Jesus is the dwelling place of God. Jesus replaces the Jerusalem temple. Jesus is the bridge between heaven and earth. Jesus is the great debunker of every claim that sins can be forgiven and God can be worshiped apart from him.

EATING HIS LAST MEAL

Jesus' Open Meals

A t the center of the church's worship stands a meal variously called communion, eucharist, mass, or the Lord's Supper. On the night when he was betrayed, Jesus charged his followers to celebrate this meal in perpetuity. Because this meal, modeled after Jesus' last supper with his disciples, is so central in the life of the church, its antecedents in Jesus' ministry are often overlooked. At one occasion, for example, Jesus has dinner at Levi's house, and "many tax collectors and 'sinners' were eating with him and his disciples" (Mark 2:15-16). On another occasion Jesus is identified as someone "who welcomes sinners and eats with them" (Luke 15:2).

Jesus' opponents find his table fellowship with tax collectors and sinners offensive. What Jesus is doing directly violates first-century Judaism's strict rules governing what to eat, how to prepare it, and with whom to eat it. Besides, sharing a meal with others was considered an expression of fellowship and intimacy. Those who ate together became bonded. To betray someone with whom one had shared a meal was considered a crime (Ps. 41:9; John 13:18).

Also keep in mind that meals were a small-scale version of societal norms and values. The social ranking prevailing in society at large also prevailed at meals: guests of the highest social status were seated next to the host; guests of the lowest status furthest from the host.

Seating people of varying ranks indiscriminately was taboo. And, of course, because sharing a meal symbolized mutual acceptance, no decent person would think of inviting a social outcast.

But Jesus turns these social norms upside down: he eats with social outcasts. By his inclusive meals he deconstructs the old world and constructs a new world. His meals shatter social boundaries and affirm equality before God. They embody his vision of how things are going to be when the kingdom of God fully arrives.

To grasp the full meaning of Jesus' open meals we must recall the meaning of the terms *sinners* and *tax collectors*. The term *sinners* used in combination with *tax collectors* does not refer to people who break God's commandments. Had Mark (in 2:15-16) used the word in that sense, he would have written that Jesus was seen eating with tax collectors and *other* sinners. Rather, Mark uses the word *sinners* in a technical sense to refer to people who, in the eyes of the Pharisees, are religiously inferior because of their ignorance of the Pharisaic tradition. They are not called sinners because they violate the law but because they do not adhere to the Pharisaic interpretation of the law. And what set tax collectors apart from all other despised groups was their continual contact with Gentiles. Living holy lives required separation from Gentile uncleanness.

Revival at Communion

"In our Scottish tradition the great revivals have often taken place in connection with the celebration of the Lord's Supper . . . where the call for repentance and faith is followed by Communion in the body and blood of Christ in which we stretch our empty hands to receive the bread and wine: 'Nothing in my hands I bring, simply to the cross I cling.' . . . In far too much preaching of Christ the ultimate responsibility is taken off the shoulders of the Lamb of God and put upon the shoulders of the poor sinner, and he knows well in his heart that he cannot cope with it."

—Thomas F. Torrance, *Preaching Christ Today*, Grand Rapids, Mich.: Eerdmans Publishing Company, 1994, p. 34ff.

Both tax collectors and "sinners" were social outcasts. Jesus' eating with them, therefore, has far-reaching social implications. The Pharisees see his behavior as a rejection of their vision of Jewish society as a people holy to the Lord. By their definition, meals must be exclusive. But by Jesus' definition, meals must be inclusive, for in this way Jesus offers acceptance and therefore forgiveness to the guests. Implicit in eating a common meal is an understanding of God as graciously embracing even the outcasts. Open table fellowship is a symbolic way of proclaiming God's forgiveness. It is an offer of salvation to guilty sinners. It turns a meal into an amnesty.

Jesus' inclusive meals were a significant part of Jesus' proclamation as a whole. Their basic role, Hans Kueng says, is frequently overlooked. These meals are signs of the coming kingdom. They offer grace and forgiveness in advance. Jesus' last supper with his disciples can be properly understood only against the background of his many meals with tax collectors and sinners (*On Being a Christian,* New York: Doubleday & Company, 1976, p. 323). These open meals proclaim forgiveness. But Jesus' last meal proclaims the *ground* of that forgiveness.

In the rest of this chapter we will examine the gospels' four distinct accounts of Jesus' last supper.

Mark's Version of Jesus' Last Meal (Mark 14:12-26)

The Passover

In Mark the last supper is a Passover meal. Jesus uses this traditional meal as a frame for his words and as a context for doing something new. Exodus 12:26-27 enjoins Jesus as the head of the family to interpret the meaning and the details of the Passover meal, to explain why unleavened bread, bitter herbs, and a roast lamb are eaten on this night. Exodus says, "When your children ask you, 'What does this ceremony mean to you?' then tell them, 'It is the Passover sacrifice to the Lord, who passed over the houses of the Israelites in Egypt and spared our homes when he struck down the Egyptians.'" Accordingly, Jesus, as head of his family of disciples, explains the meaning of the bread and wine as part of the Passover liturgy.

Between Betrayal and Desertion

How does the last supper begin in Mark? It begins with Jesus' words, "one of you will betray me" (14:18). How does it end? It ends with his words, "You will all fall away" (14:27). Between Jesus' two announcements he institutes what today we call the Lord's Supper. These announcements are pincers that painfully press home the liberating truth that "God demonstrates his own love for us in this: While we were still sinners, Christ died for us"

(Rom. 5:8). Mark brackets Jesus' filial (from the Latin word *filius,* meaning "son") faithfulness between Judas' betrayal and the disciples' fickle faithfulness. This context must have hit home in the persecuted community Mark was addressing. Mark is saying, Each time you celebrate the Lord's Supper, remember Jesus' undying faithfulness to you!

For Many

In the tradition of the Passover meal, Jesus pronounces a blessing over the bread and wine. But he does more. He adds words which connect the bread and wine with his atoning death "for many" (14:24). The expression "for many" alludes to Isaiah 53:11: "The righteous one, my servant, shall make many righteous, and he shall bear their iniquities" (NRSV). By alluding to Isaiah 53:11, Jesus is indicating that he takes the part of God's suffering servant who will bear the iniquities of many. By offering his disciples the bread and the wine, Jesus offers them a share in the atoning power of his death. When Jesus blesses the wine, his words, "This is my blood of the covenant, which is poured out for many" (14:24), recall what happened in the Sinai desert centuries earlier when God made a covenant between himself and twelve Hebrew tribes. God promised them: I will be your God, and you will be my people. Then God sealed this promise with animal blood. Moses sprinkled this blood on the people and said, "This is the blood of the covenant that the Lord has made with you" (Ex. 24:8). But because animal blood lacks intrinsic power it was meant eventually to be replaced by blood that by its own power could seal God's promise permanently. At the last supper Jesus announces, My blood does that. This wine, which symbolizes my blood to be shed, seals God's faithfulness to you for all time to come.

> ### The Holiest Mystery
>
> "Again and again over the centuries the ancient drama of Holy Communion, the Eucharist, the Mass, is acted out all over Christendom. The bread is broken and eaten, the wine drunk—these symbols with all their power to move deeply, to stir up a new kind of life in the human heart. 'The me in thee. This I have promised thee.' It is the greatest promise of the Christian faith, and it is the holiest mystery."
>
> —Frederick Buechner, *The Magnificent Defeat,* New York: The Seabury Press, 1966, p. 108.

Drinking Anew

At the end of the meal Jesus makes a vow of abstinence: "I will not drink again of the fruit of the vine until that day when I drink it anew in the kingdom of God" (14:25). In other words, the next meal I will eat with you will be the messianic meal on a transfigured earth. Jesus says he will drink the wine "anew," or "new" (in the Greek, *kainon*). To be "new," writes biblical scholar Joachim Jeremias, "is the mark of the redeemed world and of the time of salvation. . . . On a transfigured earth, where the perfect communion with God will have become a reality through corporal transfiguration, Jesus will once more, as at the Last Supper, act as the Paterfamilias" (*The Eucharistic Words of Jesus*, p. 172). The Lord's Supper is a foretaste of the end-time messianic banquet. It bids us look forward to the day when we will sit at the table with Jesus.

A Hymn

When Jesus is finished speaking, he and his disciples sing "a hymn" (14:26). At the conclusion of the Passover meal it was customary to sing the second part of the Hallel, or Hymn of Praise, consisting of four or five Old Testament psalms (Ps. 114-118 or 115-118). The Hallel was sung antiphonally: one person recited the text; the others responded to each half-verse with "Alleluiah!" The Hallel psalms sing of God's faithfulness but mourn people's unfaithfulness: "the faithfulness of the Lord endures forever" (Ps. 117:2), but "All men are liars" (Ps. 116:11). When Jesus leaves for the Mount of Olives, these words are fresh on his lips and may well have been the immediate occasion for telling his disciples, "You will all fall away" (14:27). These psalms also must have encouraged Jesus to trust the God who guides through death to resurrection:

> "For you, O Lord, have delivered
> my soul from death,
> my eyes from tears,
> my feet from stumbling,
> that I may walk before the Lord
> in the land of the living."

> —Psalm 116:8-9

Mark situates the account of the Lord's Supper institution between an act of betrayal and one of wholesale desertion. This context mirrors that of Mark's own day. Under the pressure of persecution many members of the church in Rome are tempted to become unfaithful to Christ. The bread and wine assure them of Christ's faithfulness to them.

Matthew's Version of Jesus' Last Meal
(Matt. 26:17-30)

In his account of the last supper, Matthew follows Mark rather closely, as he does throughout the passion narrative. Still, shining through Matthew's modifications of Mark's account is a distinct vision of the Lord's Supper. Each time Matthew deviates from Mark he is emphasizing something that is important to him. We can identify three such emphases:

1. *Foreknowledge.* Matthew focuses attention on Jesus' foreknowledge in places where Mark does not. For example, in 26:1-5 Jesus predicts that the Son of Man will be crucified during the Passover. The chief priests and elders of the people, on the other hand, plot to avoid killing Jesus "during the feast." They fear that otherwise a riot may erupt among the people. Jesus' prediction turns out to be true. In Matthew, Jesus also demonstrates his foreknowledge right before the Passover meal when he says, "My appointed time is near."

    Furthermore, unlike Mark's Jesus, who predicts that "one of you will betray me—one who is eating with me" (14:18), Matthew's Jesus clearly identifies his betrayer: "The one who has dipped his hand into the bowl with me will betray me" (26:23). And when Judas denies that he is the one to betray him, Jesus says, "Surely, it is you." In each of these examples Matthew emphasizes Jesus' control over the events of his passion and his status as the Son of God and the Son of Man. Writes John P. Meier, "Matthew's emphasis on the foreknowledge and control of Jesus approaches the presentation of the passion in John's gospel. Jesus marches to his death with sovereign freedom" (*The Vision of Matthew,* p. 181).

2. *Obedience.* In Mark Jesus also shows foreknowledge of coming events, as for example, when he tells two of his disciples to go into Jerusalem where a man carrying a jar of water will meet them. Jesus' words demonstrate miraculous foreknowledge, since "ordinarily only women carried water in jars. It would be normal to find a man carrying a wineskin [rather than a jar]" (William L. Lane, *The Gospel According to Mark,*

Grand Rapids, Mich.: Eerdmans Publishing Co., 1974, p. 499). Mark's Jesus then proceeds to predict precisely what will follow next, how this man "will show you a large upper room, furnished and ready." In view of Matthew's emphasis on Jesus' foreknowledge we would expect him to follow Mark's description of the preparation for the Passover meal. But he doesn't. Or rather, he abbreviates it to read, "Go into the city to a certain man and tell him, 'The Teacher says: My appointed time is near. I am going to celebrate the Passover with my disciples at your house.' So the disciples did as Jesus had directed them and prepared the Passover" (26:18-19). Surprisingly, in Matthew, Jesus' miraculous foreknowledge and its exact fulfillment are excluded. Instead of the disciples finding everything just as Jesus has told them, we read that they obediently carry out all of Jesus' instructions. And although in Mark *two* of Jesus' disciples "found things just as Jesus had told them," in Matthew *all* of Jesus' disciples "did as Jesus had directed them." In other words, Matthew here shifts the emphasis away from Jesus' miraculous foreknowledge to Jesus' demand that his disciples obey him. This shift represents something that is distinctive to Matthew. In Mark, the disciples characteristically misunderstand Jesus' teaching and who he is (6:52; 8:21); in Matthew, the disciples understand both Jesus' teaching and who he is—and they follow and obey when he commands. Thus before the Passover, they do what they are instructed to do.

> ### Prayer During Communion
>
> "Lord, it is true that I am not worthy that you should come under my roof. Yet I am in need and desire your help and grace. So I come with no other plea except that I have heard the gracious invitation to come to your altar. I am unworthy, but you have assured me I shall have forgiveness of all sins through your body and blood which I eat and drink in this sacrament. Amen, dear Lord; your Word is true. I do not doubt it. Let happen to me whatever you say. Amen."
>
> —*Luther's Prayers*, Herbert F. Brokering, ed., Minneapolis: Augsburg, 1994, p. 76.

3. *For the forgiveness of sins.* To Jesus' words in Mark, "This is my blood of the covenant, which is poured out for many" (14:24), Matthew adds, "for the forgiveness of sins" (26:18). Comments John P. Meier, "Nowhere else does Matthew make it so clear that he views Jesus' death as an expiatory sacrifice. . . . By his sacrificial death, made accessible to the disciples in the eucharist, Jesus overcomes the powers of sin and death" (*The Vision of Matthew,* p. 184). The Lord's Supper is a means of grace by which Jesus hauls off our sins. Here Jesus acts as one who "has authority on earth to forgive sins" (Mark 9:6).

Luke's Version of Jesus' Last Meal
(Luke 22:7-38)

Luke's account of the Last Supper is three times as long as that of Mark and Matthew. Only Luke 22:14-23 parallels their account. The following three features are unique to Luke:

1. *Two cups.* Luke mentions the passing of two cups, one in 22:17 that is not related to Jesus' blood but to his drinking of wine anew in the kingdom of God, and one in 22:20 that is related to Jesus' blood. Two cups rather than one makes sense when we understand how first-century Passover meals were celebrated in Palestine. According to Joachim Jeremias, an expert on this matter, these meals consisted of four parts.

   • *The preliminary course.* A blessing is said to sanctify the feast day, the first cup of wine, and the preliminary dish of herbs. At this time the main meal is served but not eaten. The second cup of wine is poured but not yet drunk.

   • *The Passover liturgy.* In response to the question asked by the youngest boy, "Why is this night different from all other nights?" the head of the family recites the Passover liturgy in Aramaic. Then follows the singing in Hebrew of the first part of the Hallel (Ps. 113 or Ps. 113-114) and the drinking of the second cup of wine.

   • *The main meal.* A blessing is pronounced over the unleavened bread. The Passover lamb is eaten with the unleavened bread and bitter herbs. The third cup of wine, the cup "after the supper" (Luke 22:20), is blessed.

   • *The conclusion.* The second part of the Hallel (Ps. 114-118 or 115-118) is sung in Hebrew.

   In Luke the first cup (22:17) refers to either the first or the second cup of wine in the above outline. The second cup, described as the cup "after the supper" (22:20), refers to the third cup of wine. As mentioned before, Jesus only connects the second cup with his blood.

2. *In memory of me.* In Luke 22:19 Jesus asks his disciples to repeat the meal in memory of him. Just as the Jewish people were commanded

annually to remember Israel's exodus from Egypt, so Jesus now enjoins his disciples to repeat their last supper with him: "Jesus gives himself, his 'body' and his 'blood,' as a new mode of celebrating Israel's feast of deliverance. His own body and blood will replace the Passover lamb as a sign of the way God's kingdom will be realized from now on, even though its fullness will not be achieved until the eschaton" (Fitzmeyer, *Luke X-XXIV*, p. 1392).

> **Bread Broken**
>
> "The bread was broken. It *must* be broken. The loaf cannot be eaten whole. So it was a spiritual necessity, a necessity in God, that Christ should die. . . . Just as truly as food must be destroyed before it can be of use to us, so He had to be destroyed before He could savingly serve us. We must be broken ere we deeply bless . . . Without this breaking there is no redemption, no share in redemption."
>
> —P. T. Forsyth, *The Church and the Sacraments*, London: Independent Press, 1917, p. 239.

3. *Warnings and instructions.* Luke structures Jesus' last supper as an occasion for issuing warnings and instructions:

    * *Betrayal.* Instead of mentioning the presence of his betrayer at the table before the institution of the Lord's Supper the way Mark and Matthew do, Jesus delays the announcement until after the institution (22:21-23). In this way Luke not only makes clear that Judas receives the bread and wine, "but also puts in sharper focus the betrayal of Judas. Not only does he deliver Jesus to the enemy but he violates a covenant in the body and blood of Jesus" (Fred B. Craddock, *Luke*, p. 255).

    * *As one who serves.* Whereas Mark and Matthew place the disciples' dispute over greatness before Jesus' arrival in Jerusalem, Luke places it at the scene of the last supper. The question about Jesus' identity, repeatedly asked throughout the gospels, is answered in Luke as follows: "I am among you as one who serves" (22:27). By placing these words in the immediate context of the Lord's Supper, Luke increases their impact.

    * *But I have prayed for you.* One of the most profound exchanges between Jesus and Simon Peter takes place in Luke 22:31-34. Peter claims he will serve Jesus to the end: "Lord, I am ready to go with you to prison and to death." This claim appears between two sobering statements of Jesus. Not only does Jesus predict that Peter will deny him three times, but he also informs Peter that "Satan has asked to sift you as wheat." In other words, if Satan has his way, Peter's faith will be blown away like chaff. But because Jesus prayed for him, this won't happen: "I have prayed for you, Simon, that your

faith may not fail." These words lay bare the eternal background of Peter's faith. On the human level Peter's faith does fail. Three times he denies that he knows Jesus. But on the divine level Peter's faith is upheld by the faithfulness of Jesus. On the divine level Jesus, as one who serves, is with Peter to the end.

In Luke, meals and food are a more pervasive theme than in Mark and Matthew. In Luke there are references to food in every chapter. In Luke, Jesus is called "a glutton and a drunkard, a friend of tax collectors and 'sinners'" (7:34). Jesus' open meals, culminating in the Lord's Supper, proclaim that in the kingdom of God the distinctions between poor and rich, male and female, slave and free, are obsolete. Luke's meal theme, therefore, is in harmony with the theme uniting both his gospel and Acts: Jesus inaugurates a worldwide community in which the distinction between Jew and Gentile is no longer important.

John's Version of Jesus' Last Meal (John 13)

John tells the story of Jesus' last meal very differently from the other gospels. His version, found in John 13, differs from that of the other gospels in at least three respects:

1. *Chronology.* According to the first three gospels, Jesus institutes the Lord's Supper during the Passover meal with his disciples. In these gospels the evening of the Passover meal, the next morning, and the afternoon on which Jesus is crucified fall on the same sundown to sundown day—the day of the Passover. The gospel of John changes the liturgical calendar by one day. It turns the clock back (13:1; 19:31). Why? Because in John Jesus *is* the Passover lamb. In John, Jesus the Passover lamb is sentenced to die at the hour when, in the temple precincts, the Passover lambs are being slaughtered. Jesus eats his last supper at sundown at the beginning of Passover eve. Then the Jews lead Jesus from Caiaphas to Pilate (19:14) and publicly renounce him as their king. This takes place, John notes, at "about the sixth hour," that is,

about noon on the day before Passover when the slaughter of the Passover lambs takes place. John, who has previously identified Jesus as "the lamb of God who takes away the sin of the world" (1:29), has the chief priests call for Jesus' crucifixion at approximately *that* hour. Raymond E. Brown explains that, "at the moment when the Passover lambs are being slaughtered, Jesus' trial comes to an end, and he sets out for Golgotha to pour forth the blood that will cleanse men from sin (1 John 1:7). Truly, as John sees it, God has planned 'the hour' carefully" (*The Gospel According to John XIII-XXI*, p. 895ff.).

2. *Foot-washing.* Because John places Jesus' death at the time of the slaying of the Passover lambs he does not give an account of the institution of the Lord's Supper in the framework of the Passover meal. In John there is, therefore, no mention of bread, wine, eating or drinking. Instead, John makes the scene of the foot-washing the focal point of the meal. From Jesus' words to Peter it appears that John regards the washing of the disciples' feet of equal importance with the Lord's Supper. In the foot-washing Jesus "showed them the full extent of his love" (13:1). John appears to be saying that one can know Jesus as much in his action of washing feet as in his action of breaking bread. "If I do not wash you," Jesus tells Peter, "you are not in fellowship with me" (13:8, NEB). Not being in fellowship with Jesus means not sharing in his death. Jesus' foot-washing, then, points to his saving death. By washing his disciples' feet, the task of a servant, Jesus is prophesying symbolically about his coming humiliation in death. In his exchange with Peter, Jesus explains that his death is necessary for salvation (see Raymond E. Brown, *The Gospel According to John XIII-XXI*, p. 568).

> **Washing Our Feet**
>
> "[W]e want God in all God's glory, goodness and greatness. We want God in all God's majesty, power, and transcendence. We can handle that—God's remoteness. But for God to wash our feet, to put on a towel rather than a robe, to be simple bread, to be that close is embarrassing—and frightening. . . . Is God like *that*? Not in heaven, but on this earth washing feet?"
>
> —William J. Bausch, *Telling Stories, Compelling Stories*, Mystic: Twenty-Third Publications, 1991, p. 162.

3. *Eat my flesh; drink my blood.* In John 13 the eating of bread and the drinking of wine are replaced by the washing of feet. John omits the scene of the Lord's Supper institution and instead moves the foot-washing to center stage. Yet John is not completely silent about the words of institution. John is using eucharistic language in John 6, where he tells the story of the multiplication of the loaves and records Jesus' long discourse on the bread of life. In John 6:51 we hear clear echoes of the words Jesus spoke over the bread in the other gospels:

- "Take it; this is my body" (Mark 14:22).
- "Take and eat; this is my body" (Matt. 26:26).
- "This is my body given for you" (Luke 22:19).
- "I am the living bread that came down from heaven. If a man eats of this bread, he will live forever. This bread is my flesh, which I will give for the life of the world" (John 6:51).

And in John 6:53-54 we hear clear echoes of the words Jesus spoke over the wine:

- "This is my blood of the covenant, which is poured out for many" (Mark 14:24).
- "Drink from it, all of you. This is my blood of the covenant, which is poured out for many for the forgiveness of sins" (Matt. 26:27-28).
- "This cup is the new covenant in my blood, which is poured out for you" (Luke 22:20).
- "Unless you eat the flesh of the Son of Man and drink his blood, you have no life in you. Whoever eats my flesh and drinks my blood has eternal life" (John 6:53-54).

In John 6:1-15, Jesus feeds five thousand people with five barley loaves of bread. In John 6:35-59, Jesus feeds people with *himself*. Jesus says, "I am the living bread that came down from heaven. If a man eats of this bread, he will live forever" (6:51). In John, Jesus does not institute the Lord's Supper; he *is* the Lord's Supper. At the Lord's Supper we eat his flesh and drink his blood (6:54). In John, Christians do not celebrate the Lord's Supper in response to Jesus' command, "This do in remembrance of me," but in response to Jesus' offer of himself as food for eternal life. This accords with the overall theme of the gospel of John: Jesus does not offer bread from heaven; he *is* that bread. Jesus does not impart life from above; he *is* the life.

> ### What Is This?
>
> "The command, after all, was Take, eat: not Take, understand. Particularly, I hope I need not be tormented by the question 'What is this?'—this wafer, this sip of wine. That has a dreadful effect on me. It invites me to take 'this' out of its holy context and regard it as an object among objects, indeed as part of nature. It is like taking a red coal out of the fire to examine it: it becomes a dead coal. To me, I mean. All this is autobiography, not theology."
>
> —C. S. Lewis, *Letters to Malcolm: Chiefly on Prayer*, London: Geoffrey Bles, 1964, p. 136.

Mark, Matthew, Luke, and John. All four gospels invite Jesus' followers to feed on his body and blood, for only in this way can we have a part in his death and resurrection life. Yet each of the gospels formulates this invitation differently, for each filters it through the eucharistic theology of the individual writers.

GOING TO THE CROSS

Crucifixion in the Ancient World

I n the ancient Mediterranean world, crucifixion was both widespread and frequent. It was not unique to the Romans. Among the Romans, however, its victims were primarily hardened criminals, political insurrectionists, and rebellious slaves. They were stripped of all their clothing and then either nailed or bound to the cross. The particular form of crucifixion varied considerably. Writes Martin Hengel in his classic study on the subject, "All attempts to give a perfect description of the crucifixion in archeological terms are therefore in vain; there were too many different possibilities for the executioner.

Therefore, when Paul writes that he preaches Christ *crucified,* he is deeply aware that his preaching runs counter to the whole ethos of contemporary religion. For to think that the only Son of God "had died the death of a common criminal on the cross, could only be regarded as a sign of madness. The real gods of Greece and Rome could be distinguished from mortal man by the very fact that they were *immortal*—they had absolutely nothing in common with the cross as a sign of shame" (*Crucifixion,* p. 7). And Paul's Jewish audience was equally scandalized by the message of the cross. They heard it against the background of Deuteronomy 21:23, "anyone who is hung on a

---

Instrument of Execution

"Suppose you were to enter a church and find a guillotine upon the altar; or a compact model of a gas chamber replacing the Communion Table; or a statue of a blindfolded man being shot by a firing squad, in place of the baptismal font; or a gilded electric chair on the wall above the pulpit. Wouldn't you think there was something strange, if not 'sick,' about giving such attention to instruments of execution? And yet that is exactly what the cross represented in the Roman Empire of the first century. The cross was an instrument of execution—the first century equivalent of guillotine, gas chamber, firing squad, and electric chair. It was the way the state got rid of its enemies."

—Robert McAfee Brown, "The Why of the Cross," A Living Faith Pamphlet, 1966, p. 3.

tree is under God's curse," a tree being roughly suggested by the shape of the cross. To Jewish thinking, a crucified Messiah is a contradiction in terms. A crucified Messiah is a Messiah cursed by God. The message of Christ crucified, therefore, is "a stumbling block to Jews and foolishness to Gentiles" (1 Cor. 1:23). Urging people to believe in someone crucified by the Romans is inviting them to engage in a counter-cultural activity.

With such intense resistance to its message of a crucified Messiah, it's no surprise that the church's main documents—the four gospels—contain lengthy and detailed accounts of Jesus' crucifixion. Believers understood that only a blow-by-blow account of the events leading up to his crucifixion could give a satisfactory answer to the question asked over and over again: Why was Jesus crucified? Each of the four gospels explains why, again from its own unique theological perspective.

The Arrest of Jesus

Gethsemane. The name conjures up a multitude of images: Jesus' agonizing sorrow, his prayer that not his will but that of his Father be done, the sleeping disciples, Judas' treacherous kiss, the crowd delegated by the Jewish authorities to arrest Jesus, a disciple cutting off the ear of the servant of the high priest, and Jesus' rhetorical question: Seeing that day after day I taught publicly and you did not arrest me, why is it that you now come out to arrest me? What all these images have in common is that they are supplied by the first three gospels. But John's account of what happens in the garden is quite different. Note, for example, the following four items:

1. *Judas.* In John, Judas does not identify Jesus with a kiss. Judas' act of betrayal consists of guiding "a detachment of soldiers together with police from the chief priests and the Pharisees" (18:3, NRSV) to the garden. Having done that, Judas passively stands by.

2. *I am the one.* In John, Judas does not identify Jesus; Jesus identifies himself. "Jesus, knowing all that was going to happen to him, went out and asked them, 'Who is it you want?' 'Jesus of Nazareth,' they replied. 'I am he,' Jesus said" (18:4-5). The words "I am he," on the level of daily conversation, simply mean, I'm the one. But from the reaction of the soldiers we learn that Jesus' words mean much more, for they draw back and fall to the ground. Jesus' words have the power to paralyze his opposition. Jesus needs no sword to defend himself. "Put your sword away!" he orders Peter. John makes it clear that Jesus needs no defense of any kind. The arresting soldiers cannot act until they receive their orders, not from their superiors but from Jesus.

3. *Torches and lanterns.* Had Jesus wished to escape arrest he could easily have done so. The soldiers coming to arrest him carried torches and lanterns. From the garden on the Mount of Olives Jesus easily could have seen the soldiers make their way across the dark Kidron Valley. Their torches and lanterns, too, bear witness that Jesus is in control over his own arrest.

4. *Soldiers and police.* The arresting party consists of two groups: "a detachment of soldiers" and "police from the chief priests and the Pharisees" (18:3, NRSV). Only John mentions "a detachment [Greek: *speira*] of soldiers." These soldiers are under the authority of a "commander" [Greek: *chiliarchos*] (18:12). Because both *speira* and *chiliarchos* are technical military terms, there is good reason to assume that John is thinking of Roman soldiers. John, in other words, clearly distinguishes these Roman soldiers, for whom he uses technical Roman terminology, from the party sent by "the chief priests and the Pharisees" (18:3). But neither the Roman soldiers nor the Jewish police can act until they receive their orders from Jesus. Clearly, John's Jesus is not the suffering servant, as he is in Mark and Matthew, but rather the triumphant king. John's Jesus does not pray that this hour and this cup may pass from him. He does not agonize before the will of God. Not Jesus but the arresting party falls to the ground.

    The presence of Roman soldiers is a striking feature of John's account. John alone implicates Rome in Jesus' arrest. With his power over both soldiers and police, Jesus shows his power over "the representatives of the two groups who will soon interrogate him and send him to the cross" (Raymond E. Brown, *The Death of the Messiah,* vol. 1, p. 261).

The Jewish Trial

In Mark and Matthew

The arresting party leads Jesus to the high priest, the person responsible for good order in Judea in general and in Jerusalem in particular. Mark tells of a formal night trial before the Sanhedrin. The members of the Sanhedrin want to know: Is Jesus a militant who intends to destroy the temple building? Witnesses are called in and interrogated: Did or didn't Jesus claim to destroy the present temple and build a new one? The testimonies, however, do not agree. The high priest then asks Jesus, Are you the Messiah, the Son of the Blessed? Jesus answers, Not only am I the Messiah, I am also the Son of Man who at the end of time will come from God's presence to judge the world. The high priest hears only blasphemy, which in Jewish law is a capital crime. Deuteronomy 13 warns against people like Jesus. People who lead Israel astray "must be put to death" (13:15). In agreeing to the charge of being the Messiah and in claiming to be the Son of Man besides, Jesus has placed himself in the category of people condemned by Deuteronomy 13. The entire Sanhedrin then condemns Jesus as deserving to die (14:64).

Matthew follows Mark's account of the Jewish trial rather closely.

In Luke

In Luke's account Jesus has no night trial. Jesus is put on trial in the early morning: "At daybreak the council of the elders of the people, both the chief priests and teachers of the law, met together, and Jesus was led before them" (22:66). What happens in Luke's morning session is similar to what happens in the night session in Mark and Matthew, except that there are no witnesses, no charge of blasphemy, and no death sentence. In Luke the appearance before the council seems more like an interrogation than a trial. In Luke the only trial is the one by Pilate.

Why did the Sanhedrin meet at night in Mark and in the morning in Luke? There is no easy answer. Writes Raymond E. Brown, "Scholars find great difficulty in their attempts to establish a historical sequence from the diverse Gospel presentations of the interrogation of Jesus by the Jewish authorities" (The Gospel of John XIII-XXI, p. 828).

In John

As in Luke, John describes Jesus' appearance before Pilate as the only trial. There is no formal trial before the Jewish court. Although Jesus is privately interrogated by Annas, the father-in-law of Caiaphas the high priest, no mention is made of witnesses or of a formal charge. All we are told is that Annas "questioned Jesus about his disciples and teaching" (18:19). Jesus' defense is the following: I've always taught openly, never secretly. Why then question me? If you want to know what I taught, ask those who heard me. Jesus, in other words, is the accuser and Annas the accused. In John, following the interrogation Annas sends Jesus to Caiaphas, who sends him on to Pilate.

The Roman Trial

In Mark

After Jesus is led into his presence, Pilate immediately zeroes in on the political aspect of the accusations. He asks, "Are you the king of the Jews?" Jesus gives an ambiguous answer and from then on observes silence. Like the suffering servant in Isaiah 53:7, Jesus does not open his mouth, but remains silent until, at the cross, he cries out with a loud voice. Pilate, who knows that the chief priests handed Jesus over to him out of envy, is reluctant to condemn Jesus. But the crowd pressures him. Finally, Pilate hands Jesus over to be crucified (15:15).

In Matthew

Matthew follows Mark closely, but he adds two subplots that modify the portrait of Pilate. First, Pilate's wife warns him, "Don't have anything to do with that innocent man, for I have suffered a great deal today in a dream because of him" (27:19). While Jewish leaders are persuading the crowd to have Barabbas released and Jesus executed, this Gentile woman pleads Jesus' innocence and seeks his release. Just as in Matthew Gentile magi recognized baby Jesus for who he truly was (2:2), now a Gentile recognizes that Jesus is innocent: "Matthew continues to show that the Gentiles are more receptive to salvation than are the Jews. Reflecting the conflict of Christianity and Judaism in Matthew's community, these scenes lead to Jesus' final commission to 'make disciples of all nations' (28:19)" (Stephen J. Binz, *The Passion and Resurrection Narratives of Jesus,* p. 58).

Second, Pilate washes his hands and declares, "I am innocent of this man's blood" (27:24). Pilate, like his wife, recognizes Jesus' innocence. But all the people answer, "Let his blood be on us and on our children!" This response echoes Old Testament texts that speak of collective guilt for shedding innocent blood—for example, Jeremiah 26:15, "If you put me to death, you will bring the guilt of innocent blood on yourselves and on this city and on those who live in it." In the end, although Pilate and his wife are favorable to Jesus, both Jews and Romans reject him.

In Luke

Unique to Luke's account is Pilate sending Jesus to Herod. Herod, king of Galilee, is in Jerusalem for the feast. Pilate sends Jesus to Herod after he learns that Jesus is a Galilean and therefore falls under Herod's jurisdiction. But Herod, after finding no basis for a charge against Jesus, sends him back to Pilate. So both a king and a governor agree on Jesus' innocence. Luke is obviously interested in demonstrating the legal innocence of Jesus. Hence, in Jesus' trial before Pilate, the governor, not once but three times, declares no crime in him. Only because of the crowd's continuing shouting does Pilate offer the choice between Barabbas and Jesus. Later, at the crucifixion, Luke again testifies to Jesus' innocence by telling how one of the two criminals declares, "this man has done nothing wrong" (23:41), and by having the centurion confess, "Surely this was a righteous man" (23:47).

As the author of Luke-Acts, Luke depicts Jesus as the inaugurator of a worldwide community. But the community faces a formidable obstacle, for official Rome looks upon Christianity with a great deal of suspicion. Its founder has been executed under Roman law. Many of its leaders, for example, Peter, Paul and Silas, have been under Roman arrest more than once. In the face of this negative image Luke is building a defense. The cornerstone of this defense is that no Roman court has ever found Jesus or any of his leading followers guilty of criminal conduct.

In John

As we have come to expect, John's account of Jesus' trial before Pilate is quite different from that of the other gospels. In John, Jesus is not silent but answers the false charges of sedition. Nor does Jesus object to the title "the king of the Jews" when Pilate uses it. Yet the focus of the trial does not lie in refuting charges. It lies in Jesus' identity. The real reason Jesus came into the world was not to be a king but to bear witness to the truth: "for this reason I came into the world, to testify to the truth. Everyone on the side of truth listens to me" (18:37).

In the other gospels, Jesus' trial consists of three episodes: (1) Jesus is silent before Pilate's questioning; (2) Pilate seeks to release Jesus instead of

Barabbas; and (3) Pilate hands Jesus over to be crucified. In John, there are not three but seven episodes, with the scenes alternating between the inside of the palace where Pilate questions Jesus and the outside where Pilate deals with the Jews and their leaders. Seven times Pilate moves back and forth between Jesus inside and the Jewish crowd outside:

- 18:29-31 (outside): "What charges are you bringing against this man?"
- 18:33, 27 (inside): "Are you the king of the Jews?"
- 18:38-40 (outside): "I find no basis for a charge against him."
- 19:1-3 (inside): Pilate has Jesus flogged.
- 19:4-8 (outside): "I find no basis for a charge against him."
- 19:9-11 (inside): "I have power either to free you or to crucify you."
- 19:12-15 (outside): "Shall I crucify your king?"

This shuttling back and forth reflects Pilate's indecisiveness and fear. He keeps weighing his own convictions against the crowd's pressure. Jesus, on the other hand, is self-assured and above the fray—to such a degree that one can hardly speak of Pilate's trial of Jesus. Not Jesus but Pilate is on trial:

> Pilate may think he has the power to try Jesus, but he is calmly told that he has no independent authority over Jesus (19:10-11). It is not Jesus who fears Pilate; it is Pilate who is afraid of Jesus, the Son of God (19:7-8). The real question is not what will happen to Jesus who controls his own destiny, but whether Pilate will betray himself by bowing to the outcry of the very people he is supposed to govern (19:12).
>
> —Raymond E. Brown, *Crucified Christ in Holy Week,* Collegeville: The Liturgical Press, 1986, p. 61.

In John, who has a different "liturgical calendar" from the other gospels, Pilate hands Jesus over to be crucified at the very hour when the Passover lambs begin to be slaughtered in the precincts of the temple. While thousands of Passover lambs are being killed, "the Lamb of God, who takes away the sin of the world" (1:29) sets out for Golgotha.

Jesus' Crucifixion

Simon of Cyrene

On the way to the place called Golgotha, a man from Cyrene by the name of Simon is forced to carry Jesus' cross. Mark identifies him as the father of Alexander and Rufus (15:21), perhaps because these two men were known

Though We Crucified Him

"The cross constantly reminds us that God comes to us even in our rejection of him. It constantly says to us that God reaches out to us even in the worst thing mankind can do or has ever done, the rejection of the grace itself. Though we crucified him when he came to us in Christ, God speaks to us still, even in that crucifixion: I do love you still. There is the 'no escape.' We rejected him; we killed him. And in that rejection and in the killing he comes to us. Nothing can separate us from the love of God, the awe-ful, terrible love of God."

—J. A. Sanders, *The Old Testament in the Cross,* New York: Harper and Brothers, 1961, p. 111.

to the community for which Mark wrote. Matthew does not mention either name. Luke describes Simon as the model disciple who carries the cross "behind Jesus" (23:26). John, however, does not mention Simon at all. John's Jesus carries his cross all the way to Golgotha (19:17). By omitting the Simon incident John focuses more sharply on the triumphant character of Jesus' passion. Jesus goes to his death, not as victim but as victor. Jesus continues to have the initiative until the very last moment, when he bows his head and gives up his spirit.

Seven Last Words

Because Matthew follows Mark very closely in the passion story, we are, for comparative purposes, left with three accounts: the gospels of Mark, Luke, and John.

Let's first identify the "words" Jesus speaks from the cross in each gospel and then discuss the features of each gospel's portrait. In Mark, Jesus speaks only one word from the cross: "My God, my God, why have you forsaken me?" (15:34). Luke has three words: "Father, forgive them, for they do not know what they are doing" (23:34), "I tell you the truth, today you will be with me in paradise" (23:43), and "Father, into your hands I commit my spirit" (23:46). In John, Jesus utters these three words: "Dear woman, here is your son. . . . Here is your mother" (19:26-27), "I am thirsty" (19:28), and "It is finished" (19:30).

We are so used to saying that Jesus spoke seven words from the cross that our first reaction is surprise at realizing that Mark only records one. To understand why, recall that in Mark Jesus is depicted as the suffering servant. Jesus' lifelong role as the suffering servant reminds us of how the book of Hebrews describes Jesus' suffering: "During the days of Jesus' life on earth, he offered up prayers and petitions with loud cries and tears to the one who could save him from death, and he was heard because of his reverent submission. Although he was a son, he learned obedience from what he suffered" (5:7-8). Jesus had to learn obedience in the three-hour darkness. He had to learn obedience while God remained silent. Thus the scene of the crucifixion is one of abandonment. Jesus hangs on the cross for six hours, three of which are filled with mockery and insults and three of which are spent in darkness. Still, the crucifixion scene is not entirely one of unrelieved abandonment, for Mark subtly invites his readers to view the scene through the filter of the entire twenty-second psalm:

- 22:1: "My God, my God, why have you forsaken me?" (see Mark 15:34)
- 22:7: "All who see me mock me; they hurl insults" (see Mark 15:29-30)
- 22:18: "They divided my garments among them and cast lots for my clothing" (see Mark 15:24)

Though the psalmist believes that God has cast him off and he experiences hell on earth (22:1-11), and though he describes the slow torture that his enemies inflict on him (22:12-21), in the end, light breaks through the dark clouds of his agony. A vision unfolds before his eyes. He sees God's world-wide kingdom: "All the ends of the earth will remember and turn to the Lord, and all the families of the nations will bow down before him, for dominion belongs to the Lord and he rules over the nations" (22:27-28). With his portrayal of the crucified Jesus as the suffering servant, Mark meant to bolster the spirit of the persecuted church in Rome. His message to them was: You must be equally obedient to the end and draw comfort from the final vision of Psalm 22.

We Preach Christ Crucified

"One of the dangers of being in church as often as I am is that it all starts to make sense. You speak of the Christian faith so casually and effortlessly that you begin to think, 'Fine thing, this Christianity. Makes good sense.' If you are not careful, you'll find yourself believing all sorts of things in church that you wouldn't dare let anyone put over on you in the real world. That which people would choke on in everyday speech, they will swallow hook, line, and sinker if it's in a sermon. That's a blessing for those of us who get paid to preach Christ crucified."

—William H. Willimon, On a Wild and Windy Mountain, Nashville: Abingdon Press, 1984, p. 65.

Luke presents a different view of the crucifixion. He portrays the crucified Jesus the way he portrays him throughout his gospel, as reaching out to all those around him. Thus Jesus prays down forgiveness on his executioners and promises Paradise to one of the criminals. His final words are not those of abandonment but of trust. He dies with the peaceful words of Psalm 31:5 on his lips: "Into your hands I commit my spirit."

In John, Jesus' cross is his throne, and his crucifixion is his enthronement. Even from the cross Jesus continues to have the initiative. He takes responsibility for his mother and the disciple whom he loves. He loves them to the end: "Here is your son," he says to the one, and "Here is your mother," he says to the other.

The brevity of John's crucifixion scene is striking. Compared to the other gospels, many things are missing: the multitude, passers-by, taunts and mockery, conversation with the two criminals, darkness, earthquake, and rending of the temple curtain. There is, instead, the mention of Scripture being fulfilled, the reminder that things are happening according to a plan. Thus, "knowing that all was now completed, and so that the Scripture would be fulfilled, Jesus said, 'I am thirsty'" (19:28). Jesus' drinking of the wine vinegar fulfills Psalm 69:21, "They . . . gave me vinegar for my thirst." John alone mentions the "stalk of the hyssop plant" used to give Jesus the wine vinegar. Hyssop, Stephen J. Binz reminds us, "was used to sprinkle the saving blood of the Passover lamb in Exodus 12:22. John evokes Old Testament symbolism to show that the blood of Jesus establishes a new covenant. Crucified at the time the paschal lambs were being slaughtered in the temple, the dying Jesus is shown to be the 'Lamb of God who takes away the sin of the world'" (*The Passion and Resurrection Narratives of Jesus,* p. 113). Jesus' final words, "It is finished," express the completion of his mission. As the one coming from the Father and being sent by the Father Jesus has completed his mission.

Mark portrays the crucified Jesus as the suffering servant, to encourage the suffering Christians in Rome. Luke, in keeping with the Luke-Acts theme that Jesus brings salvation to the whole world, portrays the crucified Jesus as reaching out to others. John portrays the crucified Jesus as the King who reigns from the cross. Reading these three crucifixion accounts, we cannot help but wonder, Which is more correct? Which is the real picture? But the answer must be: All three are equally correct, for all three are equally "God-breathed" (2 Tim. 3:16). No single account can exhaust the meaning of what took place on Golgotha. Writes Raymond E. Brown, "It is as if one walks around a large diamond to look at it from three different angles. A true picture of the whole emerges only because the viewpoints are different" (*A Crucified Christ in Holy Week,* Collegeville: The Liturgical Press, 1986, p. 70ff.).

What Frightens

"The wondrous theme of the Bible that frightens so many people is that the only visible sign of God in the world is the cross. Christ is not carried away from earth to heaven in glory, but he must go to the cross. And precisely there, where the cross stands, the resurrection is near; even there, where everyone begins to doubt God, where everyone despairs of God's power, there God is whole, there Christ is active and near. Where it is on a razor's edge, whether one becomes faithless or remains loyal—there God is, and there Christ is."

—Dietrich Bonhoeffer, *A Testament to Freedom,* Geffrey B. Kelly and F. Burton Nelson, ed., HarperSanFrancisco, 1990, p. 211.

RISING FROM DEATH

Problems, Problems

When we compare the resurrection stories of the four gospels, we soon discover what has puzzled readers throughout the centuries: how difficult it is to integrate the events of Easter Sunday as narrated in Mark 16, Matthew 28, Luke 24, and John 20. Here are a few examples:

1. *Women.* In Mark, three women go to the tomb on Easter morning: Mary Magdalene, Mary the mother of James, and Salome. In Matthew, there are only two women: Mary Magdalene and "the other Mary," presumably Mary the mother of James mentioned by Mark. Salome is not mentioned. In Luke, the number of women has increased: Mary Magdalene, Joanna, Mary the mother of James, and "the others with them" (24:10). John only mentions Mary of Magdala.

2. *Angels.* In Mark, inside the tomb, the women find "a young man dressed in a white robe sitting on the right side" (16:5) who addresses them. In Matthew, outside the tomb, the women are addressed by an angel of the Lord whose appearance is like lightning and whose clothes are as white as snow. In Luke, "two men in clothes that gleamed like lightning" (24:4) speak to the women. In John, there are "two angels in white,

seated where Jesus' body had been, one at the head and the other at the foot" (20:12).

3. *Appearances.* In Mark 16, the risen Jesus doesn't appear to anyone. In Matthew 28, he appears to the women in Jerusalem and to the disciples in Galilee. In Luke 24, he appears only in and around Jerusalem. In John 20, he appears to Mary of Magdala and to the disciples in Jerusalem.

4. *Go and tell.* In Mark, the women hurry from the tomb and say nothing to anyone. In Matthew, they tell the disciples. In Luke, they tell the Eleven and all the others. In John, Mary Magdalene reports to Simon Peter "and the other disciple, the one Jesus loved" (20:2).

Why are there so many differences? Why is it so impossible to form a consistent picture of the Easter events? We could say, with N. T. Wright, that in a great many cases "this is what eyewitness testimony looks and sounds like. And in such cases the surface discrepancies do not mean that nothing happened; rather, they mean that the witnesses have not been in collusion" (*The Meaning of Jesus*, p. 121ff.). This is a valuable insight. But it is not the whole story. More is going on here than a natural conflict of testimony by eyewitnesses overwhelmed by the magnitude of what they saw and heard. Again, we must keep in mind that the gospels, written several decades after Jesus' resurrection, were meant for specific audiences and purposes. Each writer incorporated original eyewitness testimony into his gospel to reflect a distinctive perspective on Jesus' resurrection. In other words, here again the differences among the resurrection accounts are the result of these varying perspectives. In this chapter we will take a close look at the four resurrection chapters and examine the distinguishing features of each.

Jesus' Resurrection in Mark 16

Short and Long Ending

The account of Jesus' resurrection in Mark is brief and surprisingly abrupt. Mark's short ending has evoked much discussion. What is the end of Mark's gospel? Mark 16:8 or Mark 16:20? The New International Version (as well as other Bible versions) prints the short ending, Mark 16:1-8, and also adds another ending, Mark 16:9-20—but not before informing readers that the two most reliable Greek manuscripts do not contain Mark 16:9-20. Omitting verses 9-20 is not surprising, for they contain vocabulary and themes unlike the rest of the gospel. The passage is a collage of resurrection scenes found in the other gospels. Thus, for example,

- Mark 16:12-13 = Luke 24:13-35
- Mark 16:14-16 = Matthew 28:16-20
- Mark 16:19 = Luke 24:50-51

The long ending of Mark, made familiar through the King James Version, was most likely written because Mark 16:1-8 was not understood as an ending. Frustrated readers asked: Why does Mark end so abruptly at verse 8? Why don't the women say anything to anyone? And why aren't there any appearances of the risen Jesus? These and other questions led to the composition of Mark 16:9-20.

Readers of Mark today are equally frustrated with Mark's short account of the resurrection and its strange ending. We too tend to read Mark through the glasses of, for example, Matthew's gospel—where the women *do* tell what they have seen. But to hear what chapter 16:1-8 is saying, we must set aside the other Easter accounts and listen to Mark's singular voice.

The Women and the Angel

In Mark the women visit the tomb to anoint Jesus' body. They come to perform services that have been skipped the previous Friday under the pressure of time. For to meet the Sabbath deadline at sundown on Friday, Jesus had been hastily buried. With sundown rapidly approaching, Joseph of Arimathea had gone to Pilate and asked for Jesus' body. After making sure that Jesus was indeed dead, Pilate had granted Joseph's request. Joseph then "bought some linen cloth, took down the body, wrapped it in the linen, and placed it in a tomb cut out of rock" (15:46). To bury Jesus before the beginning of the Sabbath, the time-consuming ritual of anointing the body had to be omitted. It is to correct this situation that the women come to the tomb. Finding the stone rolled away they enter the tomb. What they see is "a young man dressed in a white robe on the right side" (16:5). Mark describes this messenger of the resurrection in language conventionally used in his day to describe angels. The angel is a young man. He sits on the right side—the side symbolizing blessedness. He is dressed in a white robe, the garb of heavenly beings. Mark 16:5, in other words, describes an epiphany—a divine manifestation. And it is typical of an epiphany for those who witness it to be alarmed—as the women indeed are. "Don't be alarmed," the angel says. "You are looking for Jesus the Nazarene, who was crucified. He has risen! He is not here" (16:6). The angel then charges the women to go and tell the disciples, "He is going ahead of you into Galilee. There you will see him, just as he told you." But, shaking and puzzled, the women flee from the tomb. They say nothing to anyone, because they are afraid.

Puzzle Intensified

This ending of Mark's account of the resurrection intensifies the puzzle that Mark has been describing throughout his gospel. All the main characters in his gospel are puzzled over Jesus' identity. The crowds, the scribes, Jesus' friends, relatives and disciples—they all ask: Who is Jesus? In Mark, misunderstanding, hardness of heart, and hostility are the typical responses to Jesus. So, does Mark resolve the puzzlement by showing a full reversal after Jesus' resurrection? Surprisingly, he does not. He even intensifies the mystery of Jesus. For instead of carrying out the assignment of the angel, the three women, trembling and bewildered, say nothing to anyone, for they are afraid. Mark, surprisingly, concludes his gospel at this point. Upon deeper reflection, however, we must conclude that this ending is not all that surprising; rather, it is quite in keeping with the awe and fear people have previously displayed in response to Jesus' words and works. Throughout Mark's gospel people are unable to react to Jesus fittingly. What then is so strange about the behavior of the three women on Easter morning? The women are breathless. No wonder—they've just heard what no human being has ever heard before!

> ### Easter Fear
>
> "I'm betting that Mark does a better job of expressing how many of you feel about Easter than do the more elaborate, refined, assured words of Matthew, Luke, or John. If you want the resurrection explained to you, if you want Easter done in technicolor, pounded into you in sure and certain words of earnest conviction, argued scientifically, or evoked poetically with talk of crocuses, a butterfly emerging from a cocoon, or the return of the robin in spring, forget it. The three women have only to tell, if you can get them to tell it, of Easter fear, trembling, and silence."
>
> —William H. Willimon, *The Intrusive Word*, Grand Rapids, Mich.: Eerdmans Publishing Co., 1994, p. 139.

The short ending of Mark is also fitting because it is in keeping with the discipleship theme running through the entire gospel. In Mark 1:16-20 Jesus calls disciples. In 3:13-19 he formally appoints them. In 6:7-13, after having given them authority over unclean spirits, he sends them out on a special mission. This mission marks a turning point. From now on the disciples are portrayed as failing in three respects. They fail in their under-standing of who Jesus is, in their ability to cast out evil spirits, and in their loyalty to Jesus. After their flight from the scene of Jesus' arrest, the disciples disappear from the gospel of Mark. Peter alone endures, but after denying Jesus he too disappears. Jesus is confessed to be the Son of God, not by one of his disciples but by the officer in charge of his crucifixion (15:39). It is at this precise point that Mark introduces a group of women. They appear from nowhere and take over the role that one might have expected the disciples to play. The women watch Jesus die. They watch where Jesus is buried. They go to the tomb to anoint Jesus. They are the first to hear that Jesus is risen. But, like the disciples before them, the women also fail their mission. They say nothing to anyone. Discipleship failure, Mark is saying, is total. The twelve disciples fail Jesus, but so do the three women.

What Is Mark Saying?

Mark is saying what he has been saying all along—that *all* Israel failed to perceive Jesus as the Son of God. Did Mark finish his gospel at verse 8? We have every reason to believe that he did. Still, there is a sense in which Mark left it unfinished—expecting his readers to finish it. Mark's gospel is the story of Jesus' passion. Mark needs fifteen chapters to reach the point where he can finally write, "And they crucified him" (15:24). Having reached that crucial point, Mark then, as it were, turns toward his readers and says: Now it's *your* turn to be crucified, so that with Christ you may rise to a new kind of life, for "whoever wants to save his life will lose it, but whoever loses his life for me and for the gospel will save it" (8:35). Seen in this way, the ending of Mark's gospel is a challenge to follow Jesus no matter what the cost.

Jesus' Resurrection in Matthew 28

Matthew's report of Jesus' resurrection follows Mark, but Matthew makes several changes and additions:
- In Matthew, the women come "to look at the tomb" (28:1) because the stone has been sealed and a guard posted in front of it.

- The "young man dressed in a white robe" of Mark 16:5 becomes an angel of the Lord whose appearance is like lightning and whose clothes are as white as snow.
- The angel does not sit inside but outside the tomb, upon the stone.
- The women running from the tomb *do* tell the disciples.
- The risen Jesus appears to the women and repeats the "Go and tell" and the "Go to Galilee" instructions of the angel.

Furthermore, Matthew adds two episodes:
- the story of the guards, and
- the story of the great commission.

Let's consider how adding these two stories reveals Matthew's particular context.

The Story of the Guards

The gospel of Matthew emerged from a situation of dialogue between church and synagogue. Evidence of this dialogue is present in nearly every chapter. Unquestionably one hotly debated item in this dialogue was the bodily resurrection of Jesus. The Jewish side claimed that no resurrection had ever taken place. They charged that the disciples had stolen and hidden the body of Jesus in order to deceive people into believing that Jesus had risen from the dead. The Christian side claimed that an angel of the Lord, and not the disciples, had rolled back the stone and that God had raised Jesus from the dead. That's why Matthew includes the story of the guards in his account of the resurrection. Because Matthew is addressing a community that is Gentile and Jewish, he must rebut the charge that the disciples stole the body. The story of the guards must be seen as part of the ongoing debate in the first century between church and synagogue.

The Great Commission

Matthew closes his gospel with Jesus' commissioning. Matthew, as we noted in chapter one, presents Jesus first and foremost as the teacher of the church. He structures his gospel around five teaching discourses:
- 5:1-7:27, the Sermon on the Mount
- 10:5-42, the Mission Discourse
- 13:1-52, the Parable Discourse
- 18:1-35, the Discourse on Church Order
- 24:1-25:46, the Eschatological Discourse

The risen Jesus refers to all the teachings of all these discourses when he commissions his disciples to "go and make disciples of all nations . . . teaching them to observe everything I have commanded you" (28:19-20). This commission to teach worldwide what Jesus has taught in the five discourses is the heart of Matthew's understanding of what it means to live in a world in which Jesus is risen. "Jesus has won the final victory," notes Etienne Charpentier. "Now the territory has to be occupied, so he sends his disciples to establish his victory throughout the world" (*How to Read the New Testament,* New York: Crossroad, 1981, p. 76).

Jesus' Resurrection in Luke 24

The Empty Tomb

In Luke, very early on Easter morning, the women who had come with Jesus from Galilee go to the tomb to anoint his body. They find the stone rolled away and the body missing. Inside the tomb two men in dazzling clothes speak words that sound like a rebuke: "Why do you look for the living among the dead? He is not here; he has risen! Remember how he told you, while he was still with you in Galilee: 'The Son of Man must be delivered into the hands of sinful men, be crucified and on the third day be raised again'" (24:5-7). In other words, Why come looking for the living Jesus in a tomb? Is your memory so bad? Don't you remember what he told you? Then Luke adds that upon their return to Jerusalem the women tell all they have seen and heard "to the Eleven and to all the others" (24:9). The disciples, however, don't believe a word of it and dismiss the story of Jesus' resurrection as nonsense. Just to make sure that the women's report is bogus, Peter runs to the tomb, looks in, sees the grave clothes, and then goes home mystified, "wondering to himself what had happened" (24:12).

Luke is saying that the empty tomb itself does not lead to faith in Jesus' resurrection. That faith goes far beyond saying, Hey, look! The tomb is empty! Jesus must have risen! But if the empty tomb does not lead to faith, what does? Luke answers this question in the following story, that of the Emmaus wayfarers in Luke 24:13-35. What leads to faith, Luke says, is

Christ-centered preaching of the Scriptures and celebrating Communion. The story of the Emmaus wayfarers might be called Luke's summary gospel of the resurrection. In this story Luke includes most of what he thinks needs to be said about Jesus' resurrection.

The Story of the Emmaus Wayfarers

Strikingly, when Jesus joins up with the two disciples on their way to Emmaus, they fail to recognize him. This lack of recognition is typical of all accounts of Jesus' resurrection appearances. Though Jesus returned in his body, his resurrection body is not immediately recognizable. Because Jesus has crossed over into the new creation, to see him requires more than 20/20 vision. Now the initiative has to come from Jesus. In Matthew 28:9, for example, the women recognize Jesus only after he first says, "Greetings!" In John 20:16 Jesus speaks Mary Magdalene's name before she realizes who is speaking to her. In other instances, Jesus first points to his hands or side (John 20:25-27) or to his hands and feet (Luke 24:38-39), or he overcomes the disciples' doubt by eating fish (Luke 24:42). Jesus' resurrection is not a discovery the disciples make. Rather, Jesus reveals himself to them as risen.

The Scriptures. We had hoped, the wayfarers tell the unrecognized stranger, that Jesus was the long-awaited Messiah—the one who was going to redeem Israel, but his premature death proved us wrong. In his response Jesus shows that their image of the Messiah is more the product of popular wishful thinking than of the Old Testament revelation. Only after Jesus takes them on a tour through the Old Testament are their eyes prepared to recognize Jesus: "And beginning with Moses and all the Prophets, he explained to them in all the Scriptures concerning himself" (24:27). After his death Jesus, in their eyes, had disappeared. Now he comes walking back into their lives on the pages of the Old Testament. To see Jesus, then and now, the Old Testament light must first shine on him.

The breaking of the bread. Taking bread, blessing it, and breaking it is something the head of a Jewish family did before each meal. Because the disciples considered Jesus to be their head, taking bread, blessing, and breaking it was something Jesus did each

Glimmers of Christ

"[T]his is the substance of what I want to talk about: the clack-clack of my life. The occasional, obscure glimmering through of grace. The muffled presence of the holy. The images, always broken, partial, ambiguous, of Christ. If a vision of Christ, then a vision such as those two stragglers had at Emmaus at suppertime: just the cracking of crust as the loaf came apart in his hands ragged and white before in those most poignant words of all scripture, 'He vanished from their sight'—whoever he was, whoever they were. Whoever we are."

—Frederick Buechner, *The Alphabet of Grace,* New York: The Seabury Press, 1970, p. 8.

time they ate together. This simple, daily custom took on deeper meaning on the night before Jesus' crucifixion. On that night Jesus, as usual, "took bread, gave thanks and broke it" (22:19), but before distributing it he said, "This is my body given for you; do this in remembrance of me." In this way table fellowship was deepened to a communion between Jesus and those for whom he died. It is this deeper fellowship we witness in Luke 24:30. As soon as the three sit down at table, Jesus, though he is the guest and not the host, claims the prerogative of the head and breaks and distributes the bread. And in this familiar act Jesus reveals himself. Although on other occasions the risen Jesus identifies himself by speaking a name or by eating a piece of broiled fish, here he does it by presiding at the evening meal and changing it into the Lord's Supper.

Marked Off by Worship

Luke begins his gospel with acts of worship:

- Mary sings, "My soul praises the Lord" (1:46-47).
- Zechariah sings, "Praise be to the Lord, the God of Israel" (1:68).
- The angels sing, "Glory to God in the highest" (2:14).

Luke also ends his gospel with worship. After the resurrection and ascension, the disciples "stayed continually at the temple, praising God" (24:53). Luke's entire gospel is marked off by acts of worship. Everything in between—Christ's passion, death and resurrection—can only be believed in the context of worship, that is, in the context of Scripture proclamation and Communion celebration. Worship is the condition for recognizing Jesus and communing with him.

Jesus' Resurrection in John 20

Basic Theme

The theme that binds all of John's gospel together is that Jesus brings life. The healing of the sick (chapters 4-5), the feeding of the hungry (chapter 6), the giving of sight to the blind (chapter 9), the raising of Lazarus (chapter 11)—all are manifestations of the life-bringing ministry of Jesus. "I have come," Jesus says, "that they may have life, and have it to the full" (10:10). And Jesus' life-bringing mission reaches its climax in his death and resurrection. Here life is released in all its fullness.

John's entire gospel moves toward Jesus' death and resurrection. This explains why the gospel stories are sprinkled with the words *not yet*: "My hour has not yet come" (2:4); "The right time for me has not yet come" (7:6, 8); "his time had not yet come" (7:30); "Jesus had not yet been glorified" (7:39). But when Jesus dies, life is fully manifested, for the life he brings is like that of a grain of wheat: "Unless a kernel of wheat falls to the ground and dies, it remains only a single seed. But if it dies, it produces many seeds" (12:24). The life Jesus brings, then, is life released by his death. In John, therefore, Jesus' death is not a defeat needing a resurrection to reverse it. Rather, his death is a victory quickly followed by his resurrection, the seal of victory. To John, Jesus' death and resurrection are a single victory. He sees Jesus already as victor on the cross: "'I, when I am lifted up from the earth [onto the cross], will draw all men to myself.' He said this to show the kind of death he was going to die" (12:32-33).

> **Christus Imperator**
>
> "Why, three hundred years after the crucifixion of Jesus Christ, did the Roman emperor make peace with the Christians? Why did the mightiest man in the world capitulate to the Christian confession? Because the one to whom the emperor capitulated was Jesus Christ himself. Why was the witness to the divine truth, silenced a hundred times, not utterly destroyed? Because it was the self-witness of Jesus Christ, who was dead and is alive for evermore. Why could the Christian witness not be extirpated? Because the Crucified and Risen Lord is not an idea, but a reality, and a power which is not of this world, and which cannot be driven from the world by any power of man or subtlety of the devil."
>
> —Ethelbert Stauffer, *Christ and the Caesars*, Philadelphia: The Westminster Press, 1955, p. 220ff.

Believing Without Seeing First

In John, after Mary finds the tomb empty she runs to Peter and the other disciple, "the one Jesus loved," and gives them the news: "They have taken the Lord out of the tomb" (20:2). Both disciples run to the tomb. The disciple whom Jesus loved arrives first. He bends over, looks in, but does not go in. Then Peter arrives and enters the tomb first, followed by the other disciple. What do they see? The strips of linen and the head cloth folded up by itself, separate from the linen. Jesus' body is absent from the tomb, but clearly it has not been stolen. How does Peter react? He observes (Greek: *blepo*). How does the other disciple react? He perceives (Greek: *theoreo*) and believes. The beloved disciple does not see what he expects to. He expects to see evidence of grave robbery—grave cloths ripped off to get at the expensive spices. He perceives and believes that Jesus rose from the dead—without having seen the risen Jesus. And that, to Jesus, is faith as it should be: "blessed are those who have not seen and yet have believed" (20:29).

Jesus Appears to His Disciples

On the evening of Easter Sunday, when the disciples are together behind locked doors, Jesus comes and stands among them and says, "Shalom!" The scene that follows in John reads like a description of an early Christian worship service. It has all the basic liturgical elements:

- The disciples are gathered on Sunday, the "first day of the week" (20:19).
- Jesus himself is present.
- Jesus pronounces a blessing, twice: "Peace be with you!" (20:19, 21).
- Jesus commissions: "As the Father has sent me, I am sending you" (20:21).
- The Holy Spirit descends: "Receive the Holy Spirit" (20:22).
- Jesus promises forgiveness: "If you forgive anyone his sins, they are forgiven; if you do not forgive them, they are not forgiven" (20:23).
- A week later, when Thomas is also present, Jesus is confessed as Lord and God (20:28).

The John 20:19-28 passage links resurrection to worship. The risen Jesus is the worshiped Jesus. No one can hope to commune with the risen Jesus and stand aloof from the worshiping community, as Thomas found out.

Thomas's Doubt

Thomas has skipped church on Easter Sunday. Told about Jesus' appearance, he replied, "Unless I see the nail marks in his hands and put my finger where the nails were, and put my hand into his side, I will not believe it" (20:25). Thomas is looking for evidence. Unless my hands and eyes convince me, he says, I refuse to believe. A week later when Jesus appears again he includes Thomas in his greeting. Jesus' answer to Thomas' doubt is, "Put your finger here; see my hands. Reach out your hand and put it into my side" (20:27). Comments Austin Farrer, "They are more blessed, said Christ, who do not need such brutal evidence as the exploring of wounds with a finger. . . . Nevertheless, Christ had mercy on St. Thomas, he acknowledged the honesty of his disbelief, and took extreme measures to meet and overcome it" (*The End of Man*, Grand Rapids, Mich.: Eerdmans Publishing Co., 1973, p. 16ff.). Jesus' reply to Thomas was especially relevant to the Christians for whom John wrote his gospel around the end of the first century. All the eyewitnesses of the resurrection were dead. With their passing the church had lost its direct contact with Jesus. Then were those who had not seen the risen Jesus at a disadvantage? Not at all, John's Jesus is saying. The fact that I did not appear to you does not in any way make you inferior to those to whom I did appear. For the Spirit of truth has come to you now. The Spirit takes the place of the original eyewitnesses. The Spirit brings "glory to me by taking what is mine and making it known to you" (16:14). You who are living now are on the same level of blessedness with those who were living then: "Blessed are those who have not seen and yet have believed" (20:29).

Summing Up

The story of Jesus' resurrection is not an eyewitness report of the resurrection itself. It is unlike the story of the resurrection of Lazarus. In John 11 we are there when the stone is taken away. We are there when Lazarus comes out of the tomb, "his hands and feet wrapped with strips of linen, and a cloth around his face." We are there when Jesus says, "Take off the grave clothes and let him go." But things are different in the story of Jesus' resurrection. The resurrection takes place out of our sight. Jesus has already left the tomb by the time the women arrive. But we do see angels who tell us that Jesus is no longer dead. They report that Jesus has crossed over from death to life. Also, we have testimonies of people who saw the risen Jesus. Their testimony is unanimous: Jesus lives. In addition, we have received the Spirit of truth who bears witness that Jesus lives.

As we have seen, the four accounts of Jesus' resurrection are far from unified. The differences between them reflect the bewilderment that Easter morning brought. They testify to the radical honesty of the early church, for rather than smooth out these differences the church allowed them to stand. But what remains beyond doubt, in spite of these differences, is the unanimity of the early church's confession: It is true! The Lord has risen!

AFTERWORD

We have completed our journey through the four gospels. We have discovered that God spoke "in many and various ways" (Heb. 1:1, NRSV) through the gospel writers—just as God spoke through the prophets. The gospels, we could say, are frontier documents. Originating as part of the movement that carried the good news into the Greek-Roman world, they were born in a situation of conflict and controversy and persecution. They were not written first of all to keep an exact record of the things Jesus said and did. Their first aim is to convey the message "that Jesus is the Christ, the Son of God, and that by believing you may have life in his name" (John 20:31). But this single message is colored and shaped by the different frontier situations. Each of the gospels filters what Jesus said and did through a different set of experiences. Second-century Tatian—and others—have assumed that Christians need a single harmonized story of Jesus. The church, guided by the Holy Spirit, has chosen another way. The church has decided to let Mark be Mark, Matthew be Matthew, Luke be Luke, and John be John. By rejecting Tatian's harmony of the four gospels and embracing the four gospels with all their divergences, the church is saying that the reality of the crucified and risen Jesus is more profound and complex than the portrait of Jesus in any single gospel—or, for that matter, more profound and complex than the portraits of all four gospels together. After all, Jesus is "the image of the invisible God" in whom "all the fullness of God was pleased to dwell" (Col. 1:15, 19, NRSV).

BIBLIOGRAPHY

The author acknowledges varying degrees of indebtedness to the following works, many of which are quoted or described in the text of this book.

Binz, Stephen J. *The Passion and Resurrection Narratives of Jesus: A Commentary.* Collegeville, Minn.: The Liturgical Press, 1989.

Borg, Marcus J. *Meeting Jesus Again for the First Time.* San Francisco: Harper, 1994.

_____. *Conflict, Holiness and Politics in the Teaching of Jesus.* Harrisburg: Trinity Press International, 1998.

Borg, Marcus J. and N. T. Wright. *The Meaning of Jesus: Two Visions.* San Francisco: Harper, 1999.

Bornkamm, Guenther. *Jesus of Nazareth.* New York: Harper & Row, 1960.

Brown, Raymond E. *New Testament Essays.* Milwaukee: Bruce Publishing Co., 1965.

_____. *The Gospel According to John, vols. 1 and 2.* New York: Doubleday, 1966, 1970.

_____. *The Birth of the Messiah.* New York: Doubleday, 1977.

_____. *The Death of the Messiah, vols. 1 and 2.* New York: Doubleday, 1994.

Crossan, John D. *The Dark Interval*. Allen, Tex.: Argus Communications, 1975.

_____. *In Parables*. Sonoma, Calif.: Polebridge Press, 1992.

Davies, W. D. *Invitation to the New Testament*. New York: Doubleday, 1966.

Fitzmyer, Joseph A. *The Gospel According to Luke, vols. 1 and 2*. New York: Doubleday, 1981, 1985.

Fuller, Reginald H. *Interpreting the Miracles*. Philadelphia: Westminster Press, 1963.

_____. *The Formation of the Resurrection Narratives*. Philadelphia: Fortress Press, 1980.

Hengel, Martin. *Crucifixion*. Philadelphia: Fortress Press, 1977.

Jeremias, Joachim. *The Eucharistic Words of Jesus*. New York: The MacMillan Company, 1955.

_____. *Rediscovering the Parables*. New York: Charles Scribner's Sons, 1966.

_____. *New Testament Theology*. New York: Charles Scribner's Sons, 1971.

Juel, Donald H. *A Master of Surprise*. Minneapolis: Fortress Press, 1994.

Kodell, Jerome. *The Eucharist in the New Testament*. Collegeville, Minn.: The Liturgical Press, 1991.

Kysar, Robert. *The Maverick Gospel*. Atlanta: John Knox Press, 1976.

_____. *John's Story of Jesus*. Philadelphia: Fortress Press, 1984.

Lightfoot, R. H. *The Gospel Message of St. Mark*. Oxford: Clarendon Press, 1950.

Lohmeyer, Ernst. *Lord of the Temple*. London: Oliver and Boyd, 1961.

Meier, John P. *The Vision of Matthew*. New York: Crossroad, 1979.

_____. *A Marginal Jew, vols. 1 and 2*. New York: Doubleday, 1991, 1994.

Morris, Leon. *Apocalyptic*. Grand Rapids, Mich.: Eerdmans Publishing Co., 1972.

Perrin, Norman. *Rediscovering the Teaching of Jesus*. New York: Harper & Row, 1976.

_____. *Jesus and the Language of the Kingdom*. Philadelphia: Fortress Press, 1976.

_____. *The Resurrection According to Matthew, Mark, and Luke*. Philadelphia: Fortress Press, 1977.

Reicke, Bo. *The Gospel of Luke*. Richmond: John Knox Press, 1964.

Rhoads, David. "Losing Life for Others in the Face of Death," in *Interpretation*, October 1993, pp. 358-369.

Richardson, Alan. *The Miracle-Stories of the Gospels.* London: SCM Press, 1952.

Ridderbos, Herman N. *The Coming of the Kingdom.* St. Catharines, Ont.: Paideia Press, 1962.

Sanders, E. P. *Jesus and Judaism.* Philadelphia: Fortress Press, 1985.

_____. *The Historical Figure of Jesus.* New York: Penguin Books, 1993.

Schnackenburg, Rudolf. *Jesus in the Gospels.* Louisville: Westminster John Knox Press, 1995.

Stanton, Graham, ed. *The Interpretation of Matthew.* Philadelphia: Fortress Press, 1983.

Stauffer, Ethelbert. *Christ and the Caesars.* Philadelphia: Westminster, 1955.

Wink, Walter. *John the Baptist in the Gospel Tradition.* Cambridge: The University Press, 1968.

Wright, N. T. *The New Testament and the People of God.* Minneapolis: Fortress Press, 1992.

_____. Jesus and the Victory of God. Minneapolis: Fortress Press, 1996.